STRATEGIC SELF-HYPNOSIS

STRATEGIC SELF-HYPNOSIS

How to Overcome Stress, Improve Performance, and Live to Your Fullest Potential

by Roger A. Straus, Ph.D.

PRENTICE-HALL, INC.
Englewood Cliffs, New Jersey 07632

Dedicated, as all first books should be,
to my parents.

STRATEGIC SELF-HYPNOSIS: How to Overcome Stress, Improve Performance,
and Live to Your Fullest Potential, by Roger A. Straus, Ph.D.
Copyright © 1982 by Roger A. Straus
Address inquiries to Prentice-Hall, Inc.,
Englewood Cliffs, N.J. 07632
Printed in the United States of America

Library of Congress Cataloging in Publication Data

Straus, Roger A. (Roger Austin), date
Strategic self-hypnosis.

Bibliography: p.
Includes index.
1. Autogenic training.   2. Stress (Psycho-
logy)   3.   Success.   I.   Title.
RC499.A8S77   616.89′162   81-12155
                            AACR2
ISBN 0-13-851303-1
ISBN 0-13-851295-7 {PBK}

FOREWORD

More has been learned about hypnosis and self-hypnosis in the past twenty-five years than in the preceding two hundred years. Foreshadowed by R. W. White's influential theory in the forties and the seminal work of Sarbin in the fifties, vast strides were made both clinically and experimentally during the sixties and seventies when a "hypnosis renaissance" occurred and the fog that had so long clouded this topic began to lift. The many new understandings which have accumulated during recent decades have been beautifully integrated and extended by Roger A. Straus in this useful book, *Strategic Self-Hypnosis.*

The hypnosis renaissance of the sixties and seventies yielded at least four major insights into self-hypnosis:

1. Self-hypnosis is much broader and more important than was previously thought. Since it involves a direct attempt through goal-directed self-suggestions to change one's own feelings, thoughts, and fantasies, it can markedly change the course of a person's life.

2. Self-hypnosis can be viewed as a learnable skill; students learn how to take an active role in their own guidance, how to word goal-directed suggestions for themselves, and how to use creatively their imagination and fantasy.

3. As implied above, self-hypnosis, from the new viewpoint, refers to individuals purposively giving themselves useful goal-directed suggestions. In fact, self-hypnosis loses its aura of mystery and becomes much more applicable when one sees that it actually refers to certain types of goal-directed self-suggestions (Barber, 1978, 1979a, 1979b). A very important set of self-suggestions are those for absolute calmness and total mental-physical relaxation. These kinds of deep-relaxation suggestions, which are typically given subvocally to oneself while alone,

with eyes closed, are especially helpful for relieving stress and tension and for alleviating psychosomatic ailments. A second very important set of self-suggestions are those for active relaxation, which are to be used in ongoing daily life. Active-relaxation suggestions can be helpful throughout the day, since the individual suggests to himself or herself—while actively working, studying, performing, playing, etc.—that he or she is calm, at ease, not worried, and concentrating in a peaceful, proficient, focused manner on the immediate life situation or task. Other useful self-hypnosis procedures include self-suggestions to feel more alive, strong, healthy, energetic, and aware; self-suggestions to appreciate again and to feel deeply again both the wonderful free things of life (the sunrise, the birds, the animals, the plants, the children, the rain) and also the many miracles of our existence (seeing, hearing, feeling, thinking, imagining, dreaming, walking, talking, being conscious, being aware); self-suggestions to enjoy the flowing events of life, to have fun, and to feel good and happy again; and self-suggestions to allow our loving, kind, compassionate feelings to come forth and to feel them flowing out to others.

Dr. Straus has given examples of many of these types of self-suggestions in this text, and he has also commendably emphasized the importance of (a) letting go, "not trying," and allowing the self-suggestions to flow deeply into our mind/body, (b) combining the self-suggestions with self-guided imagery and visualization of oneself in the suggested situation, and (c) loading the self-suggestions with rich sensory details (not "I feel warmth from the fireplace" but "I feel warmth from the crackling orange and red flames, which are licking upward and sending out little showers of glowing sparks").

4. Although self-hypnosis has commonly been viewed as most useful in psychotherapeutic situations, it has even more potential in educational settings. The focus in formal education is far too much on mastering specific subject matter—mathematics, history, languages, sciences—and far too little in mastering ourselves and our own lives. Learning to block negative self-suggestions ("I can't . . ." "What if . . ." "I'm tired and bored . . .") and learning to give oneself positive goal-directed suggestions for greater enjoyment and more effective functioning should be part of formal education throughout our life span (Barber, 1979c). I expect this text by Dr. Straus will play a significant role in publicizing the vast educational potentials of strategic self-hypnosis.

Theodore X. Barber, Ph.D.
Cushing Hospital
Framingham, Massachusetts

References

Barber, T. X. *Positive Suggestions for Effective Living and Philosophical Hypnosis.* Cassette tape, Medfield, Mass. (P.O. Box 312), Medfield Foundation, 1978.

Barber, T. X. *Hypnotic Suggestions for Weight Control and Smoking Cessation.* Cassette tape, 1979. (a)

Barber, T. X. *Hypnotic and Self-Hypnotic Suggestions for Study-Concentration, Relaxation, Pain Control, and Mystical Experience.* Cassette tape, 1979. (b)

Barber, T. X. "Training students to use self-suggestions for personal growth: methods and word-by-word instructions." *Journal of Suggestive-Accelerative Learning and Teaching,* 4, No. 2 (1979), pp. 111–128. (c)

CONTENTS

PREFACE

What You Can Get From This Book

I have written this book for you to read, and also for you to use. It is an enjoyable, nontechnical introduction to scientifically proven ways of using your mind to achieve goals and to improve your performance in work, sports, study, your personal life, and in everything you do. It will teach you a method called *strategic self-hypnosis* by which you can attain full, conscious control over your mind and body.

We will cover a wide range of self-improvement objectives. Specifically, you will be learning how to relax and manage stress, how to use your full potential to meet challenges and solve problems, how to change your habits, overcome pain, control your physical state or responses, develop a more positive attitude, and program yourself for success. The techniques you will learn are based upon accepted scientific research and have been thoroughly tested in my workshops and clinical practice.

As you learn these new mental skills, you will learn a great deal about yourself, your potentialities, hypnosis, and self-hypnosis. However, this is not so much a book *about* these things as it is a book on *how to make your life work out the way you want it to.*

You could learn a great deal by simply reading through the text as you would read any other volume. Much of the information it presents has not previously been available to the general public. However, to get the most from this book, use it in the special way for which it was designed. That is, use it as a training manual. It will introduce you to practical strategies you can actually use in daily life. As you read through each chapter, you will come across a number of experiments and exercises set off from the rest of the text. When you come to one of these, stop, read, and follow the complete instructions provided. By working with these exercises, you will not only have the opportunity to check things out for yourself, but within a month's time you should be able to master the skills you'll need to make some real headway toward your personal goals.

Besides this volume, you'll need an inexpensive cassette tape recorder, three blank sixty-minute cassettes, and a spiral-bound notebook to keep as your journal. By working with your own tapes, as you will be instructed, you can obtain the same benefits as you'd get from working with your own personal counselor.

Be prepared for an exciting and pleasurable experience. You are about to discover that strategic self-hypnosis is not only an easy and effective way to learn self-control and self-improvement skills, but it is also a thoroughly enjoyable way to do so. The exercises and experiments are designed not only to instruct, but to be fun.

You are embarking upon an adventure beyond your wildest imaginations—bon voyage!

Roger A. Straus, Ph.D.
Davis, California

ONE

Hypnosis
Is Something
You Do

You are in a psychiatrist's office, reclining on a comfortable chair. The doctor is saying, "Please take this large, helium-filled balloon in your right hand. That's right. This is a special balloon—it is your own favorite color. Notice how it begins to tug at your hand and arm just like a real balloon. It is so big and light it wants to float your hand and arm right up all the way into the air. Why don't you tell me what your pretty balloon looks like to you?"

You reply in a tiny, childlike voice, "Oh, it's a red Mickey Mouse balloon." Somehow you haven't noticed that your right hand is slowly lifting off your lap. Before long, it is just hanging there in midair.

The doctor talks on about this and that. Then he interjects, "Oh, why don't you let go of your balloon now and just watch it float away into the clouds?"

Your hand opens—by itself, it seems. Then it begins very slowly to settle back into your lap. The session continues.

That's hypnosis, isn't it? Under what other circumstances would such a thing take place? A person hallucinates a red balloon which then pulls a hand into the air. Of course that's hypnosis!

What else could you think? You are reading this book because you are hoping to learn more about hypnosis and what it can do for you. Therefore, you have some notion of what hypnosis refers to. You read a scenario in which we saw a hypnotist *making* your hand do something unusual. Probably you assumed that he had first "put you into hypnosis." Isn't that why his suggestions could have such an extraordinary effect?

If that's the case, what good can reading this book do? Without somebody to hypnotize you and tell you what to do, what can you get out of it?

One heck of a lot. You see, we have a backward understanding of hypnosis. We believe hypnosis is something done to you—first you are placed into a trance state and then, if you are a good subject, you feel or think or do whatever the hypnotist suggests.

Hundreds of intelligent, otherwise well-informed people have come to me asking me to "do it to them." They seem to assume that it's something like fixing a car or programming a computer.

They seem, in other words, to have swallowed the lie that they themselves do not have the power. Rather, that they are objects like automobiles or electronic computers. This is the big lie of our era: that you are a thing, a more or less passive victim of all kinds of forces beyond your control, that you are programmed to think and act in a certain way, a sort of biological computer who needs to find a good reprogrammer.

There is a kernel of truth in this, as in most of the myths by which we are persuaded to live our lives. However, we need to address the unspoken question: Who is doing what to whom, and how?

So let's try an experiment.

Experiment One: How Does It Work?
Purpose

To gain firsthand insight into some classic hypnotic responses.

Method

Guided fantasy. You will prepare a tape-recorded script and then, as you play back your recorded instructions, you do make-believe. You don't want to think about what you are hearing, but rather to think and imagine along as if everything being said were actually happening. That's what "guided fantasy" means.

Directions

First prepare your script. Read through the script and then read it aloud, speaking in a calm, clear, natural voice. Emphasize underlined words, leave pauses where you find three dots (. . .), ham it up as you feel appropriate. Leave 30 seconds blank before and after you record your voice.

Script

"I am going to close my eyes now. I close them and let myself really *feel* how tightly shut my eyes can feel. As I let myself experience my eyes tightly closed, they begin to feel more and more tightly shut . . . as if they were stuck tight . . . very heavy, very tightly closed . . . I am going to let my eyes close *more* and *more* tightly now with every breath I breathe in and with every breath I breathe out . . . I can *feel* them closing tighter and tighter shut. . . .

"I can use my imagination to really build up this stuck-tight feeling . . . so I am imagining that someone is taking a special magic surgical glue and puts one drop on my upper eyelid and one drop on my lower eyelid, and I tell myself I can feel this glue taking effect now . . . becoming very, *very sticky* . . . gluing my eyes tightly shut .. as if they were one piece of skin . . . covering my eyes . . . glued closed now   . I let myself *really feel it* now, more and more. . . .

"To make doubly certain that my eyes feel *stuck tightly* shut, they are taking some chewing gum and working a gooey wad over my right eye and my left eye . . . really working it into my eyelashes . . . so they become all gooed up . . . very *sticky* . . . sealing my eyes *shut* . . . all gummed up . . . I can feel that my eyelid muscles feel too weak to tug my eyes open . . . they can't open against this sticky gum . . . sealed tightly shut now . . . I can *really feel it.* . . .

"And they are taking some package-sealing tape, just to make sure, and a six-inch-long strip of super-strong package-sealing tape is being stuck over my right eye now . . . and now my left eye . . . and I can feel them taping my eyes shut and I can *really* feel it . . . shut . . . sealed . . . glued and taped shut . . . I can feel my eyes stuck more and more tightly closed . . . stuck tighter and tighter with every breath I breathe in, more and more impossible to force open with every breath I breathe out . . . it feels *more* and *more* like it would be *useless* to *try* pulling my eyes open now. . . .

"My eyes are *stuck* so *very tightly* shut now . . . I can really feel it . . . feel them glued and gummed and taped shut . . . and the more I try to *force* my eyelids to open, the more they fight to stay shut . . . I can feel it more and more now . . . more and more . . . I keep thinking about and feeling this stuck-tight feeling. . . .

"While I keep on telling myself my eyes are stuck tightly closed . . . and I keep my mind thinking and feeling and picturing and imagining how they are glued and gummed and taped so they couldn't possibly open, I will try as *hard* as I can to *force* them to open anyhow. . .

"It's useless, but I will now try to force my eyelids apart . . . they feel odder and odder, the harder I try . . . I can *feel it* in my eyebrows and my forehead . . . my eyes feel glued and gummed and taped all the way shut . . . so tightly they feel numb . . . they just don't seem to want to open .   but I try to make them open anyway
     I can't . . . they're *stuck tight.* . . .

     'I try harder . . . I *strain* to force them open . . .

to *pull* my eyelids apart ... the *harder* I try the *more tightly* they stick, they just don't seem to want to open. ...

"But now I'm going to stop trying to open my eyes ... I just relax and let my eyes and my eyelids relax ... the stuck feelings all go away ... the tape and the glue and the gum feelings all go away now ... I know I can open my eyes if I just allow them to open ... all by themselves ... I just allow my eyes to pop open naturally and automatically ... the experiment is over and I can once again allow my eyes to open."

End of script. I suggest that you write the date, experiment number, and then jot down some notes in your notebook or journal: What did you experience? How did it go? What do you think was going on? How does it work?

If you experienced nothing out of the ordinary, try the experiment again. What probably happened is that you either did not allow yourself to really get into the imagining process, or else you stopped to think about it somewhere along the line. Make the script come alive for yourself by imagining as vividly and as realistically as you can. In other words, just *pretend* that you are *already experiencing* what you are suggesting to yourself.

When you do that, you'll find that you can experience some degree of eye catalepsy, as it is called. You will have difficulty or complete inability to open your own eyes. Before you go any further, repeat the experiment until you can really notice this effect—it is very important.

Catalepsy, its opposite—called levitation, as in the floating hand described earlier—hallucinations, and amnesia are all classic examples of hypnotic response. Yet you weren't hypnotized just now, were you? You didn't have to be. *Nobody was doing anything but you, yourself.*

Of course, there were some tricks involved. For one thing, we set up what is called a *double-bind* situation. You were asked to do one thing and then, while you were making your eyes feel stuck tight, you were asked to do the opposite—to open your eyes. Unless you stopped to think about it, you couldn't open them *because you were making them stay closed.* Asking you to *try* and *force* them open only compounds the effect by getting you to interfere with the mechanism by which your eyelids open. Straining often has that effect.

It's rather like judo. In this and most examples of involuntary hypnotic response, your own effort is used to create the illusion of automatic behavior. A conventional hypnotist would never clue you in to this—rather, he'd lead you to believe that your eyes weren't opening "because you were hypnotized."

That would have fit your expectations, wouldn't it? Yet the truth of the matter is that whatever happened happened because you were cooperating with the suggestions and striving to do your very best!

Hypnosis, you see, is something you do. You made your eyes stick tight because you were imagining along with your script. If you succeeded, that's because you did it correctly. If you had trouble keeping your eyes feeling stuck tightly closed, you were probably going about it the wrong way.

What, then, is the right way to go about doing hypnosis? You can start with three basic "how to do it" principles:

The First Principle: Relaxing and Letting Go. The secret of hypnosis is doing make-believe in the same way a small child goes about it. You allow yourself to ignore "reality." Forget your ideas about what is real and what isn't real, what is possible and what is impossible, what you are experiencing right now and what you are only imagining. Just let go of your grown-up's mental set, forget all the rules, and just indulge yourself. Hypnosis is a form of play. When you are doing make-believe, you don't need to worry about a thing; you can just let yourself experience it as if your fantasy were actually happening.

This can be quite difficult for us. Ever since age five or six, we have been taught that we must keep our attention in the real world. We must constantly ensure that we are in control. As I said, hypnosis is a form of play, so you can just forget about all those rules.

Easier said than done, right?

Of course. However, there's a trick you can use to let go. That trick is *relaxation.* When one's mind and body become deeply relaxed, it becomes easier to let go. It becomes natural to just drift; everyone experiences this in that period right before falling asleep.

Those readers who have indulged in recreational drugs are even more familiar with the phenomenon. Sometimes you notice it when you have made yourself tipsy. It's the rule, however, when high on marijuana—in fact, this letting go and drifting is characteristic of that particular drug. If you get high and listen to music, for example, you can enter a half-dreaming state in which you can almost lose yourself in the experience of listening.

That's precisely what you want to do in hypnosis. However, it does not help to use drugs in this case, because then it becomes too easy for you to become distracted or to get hung up on a line of spontaneous fantasy. Young children have the same sort of problem; the cost of lowering the barriers between reality and fantasy is messing up your attention span.

There's a better way—in fact, there are any number of better ways to bring about the deep mind-body relaxation that facilitates hypnotic work. These include all the relaxation techniques found in yoga, meditation, humanistic psychology practice, and everyday life. Any of these are used by somebody or other as part of a hypnosis or self-hypnosis technique. Anything that can bring about deep relaxation can help you let go. We will work with several of these techniques as we go along.

For now, just keep this principle in mind: *To successfully work with hypnotic techniques, you must begin by relaxing and letting go.* Details are not important at this point.

The Second Principle: Imagining Along With Suggestions. Once you are relaxed and letting go, you must begin doing something with your mind. Otherwise you are not doing hypnosis, but meditating or perhaps falling asleep.

The essence of hypnosis is working with suggestions; you work with suggestions by using your imagination. It's like daydreaming, only different.

When you are reading a really good story, you may find yourself practically experiencing what is going on within it. How? You take black marks printed on the paper and associate them with actual words, from which you can reconstruct the scenes and action "in your mind's eye." You experience a kind of alternate reality in the theater of your imagination.

Some people (like myself) can get so absorbed in reading that we become oblivious to the world around us. More than that, we may find ourselves laughing or crying or starting in sudden fright as the events unfold. It's almost as if we were living the story.

That's exactly what you want to do in hypnosis. You want to dramatize a story in your mind's eye. The script is supplied by the suggestions, whether you are giving them to yourself (in self-hypnosis) or listening to a tape or a live hypnotist. You take the script and make it come alive for yourself. In other words, do like a child doing make-believe.

The key concept here is *imagining* that what was being suggested was actually happening for you or to you. Now, you don't have to see or hear or actually sense anything in any way whatsoever. You need only think and feel *as if* you were doing so. Nor do you have to accept or believe what is being suggested; you merely have to go along with it *as if* these events were actually occurring.

Another thing—how you imagine things is your own affair. Only you know how things "should" look and feel to you. If I asked you, in hypnosis, to picture a very sexy person you could imagine getting romantically involved with, whatever you conjure up is perfectly correct.

In fact, the more you involve yourself in the process of building up your own subjective experience in hypnosis, the better it will work for you. That is because hypnosis is something you do. The more you put into it, the more you get out of it. Put your heart into it and you may just get out of it your heart's desire.

The Third Principle: Not Trying, but Allowing It to Happen. I already mentioned the second trick concealed in your eye catalepsy experiment—you were asked to try to open your eyes. That's simply a good way to make it difficult for yourself.

The notion of trying is a rather subtle trap. First of all, when you try to do something, you redirect your attention and your efforts away from what you are trying to do and onto all the little steps and stages involved in bringing that about. Additionally, trying is intimately bound up with the idea of *straining to make it happen.* When you try, you apply special effort, brute force. You push and you shove and you strain and you tug and you pull—anything but allow events to take their own natural course.

This is a key concept in all phases of working with yourself: When you try, you only mess things up. In the case of opening your eyes, the fact is that eyelid-opening muscles don't work when you attempt to force your eyes open. Rather, eyes open semiautomatically when you allow them to open by themselves. Let's check this out:

___

Experiment Two: Effort Versus Allowing
Purpose
    To compare two very different ways of exercising control.
Method
    Read and do—first A, then B. No need to tape-record.

Directions

A. Breathing

Close your eyes and tell yourself you are going to place your breathing under conscious control, as if switching your body from "autopilot" onto "manual control." For a couple of minutes, try to make your body breathe in a natural, relaxed fashion. Notice any difficulty. Then just relax and allow yourself to once again breathe automatically. Stop trying to control your breathing. You may find it difficult at first—if so, just close your eyes and stretch, to distract yourself. Then just allow yourself to continue breathing naturally. Compare this with what it was like to make yourself breathe.

B. Eye Opening

Close your eyes again. Now, with all your might, try to force your eyes to open. Use all the strain and effort you can. Notice what occurs. Then just allow your eyes to pop open; just let go and your eyes will open by themselves as they always have for you. How would you describe the difference between using effort and just allowing your eyes to open?

End of experiment. As for every experiment or exercise, it is a good idea to write some notes in your journal—list the date, experiment number, and then your observations and conclusions.

Do you see now how trying interferes with actually doing things? The principle applies even more strongly when working with your mind: The strain and effort of trying tends to block whatever outcome you are aiming toward. In fact, the more you try, the more your mind becomes obsessed with the problem you are trying to overcome. So you get uptight. Your mind locks up. You cannot think. You fight yourself—and you get nowhere.

That's why we use relaxation to enable you to let go. When you relax you can just allow things to happen. You need not bother to try.

For instance, every child learns you can't make yourself go to sleep. The harder you try, the more awake you become. So you learn to invent ways of distracting yourself, of lulling yourself to sleep. In effect, you learn to allow sleep to happen.

This is also how to do hypnosis. You relax, let go, and allow yourself to make believe along with the suggestions. You can't force it; you don't try.

Returning to the example of going to sleep, each of us develops our own private little rituals for this purpose. Similarly, you have your own private rituals for imagining. Some of us—again like myself—actually combine the two; I put myself to sleep by drifting into a fantasy. I know, but can't verbalize, how I do that. How do *you* turn on your imagination? When you pictured that very sexy person a few pages back, what did you do inside yourself?

Whatever you did, it was the right thing to do. When you begin working with hypnotic visualizations, go about it the same way. *Do whatever you do inside yourself to allow your imagination to function.*

This last point merits closer scrutiny. It actually combines our next four "how to do it" principles:

4. *Whatever happens, whatever you experience, that is always appropriate.*
5. *Don't worry, don't bother to think about what's happening, just let it flow.*
6. *Take an experimental "give it the old college try and see what happens" attitude.*
7. *Feel free to translate suggestions into your own words and images, add whatever's missing, or use hands and body to facilitate your imagining.*

All but this last are pretty obvious. Number seven might seem to contradict everything you ever heard about hypnosis—if so, great! The fact of the matter is that the subject is never really passive, but only looks that way because he or she is working in the world of imagination rather than the external reality. So why not make it easy on yourself?

If I have you imagine biting into a red Delicious apple and you can't stand red apples, but love sour green ones, then by all means picture a green apple instead. You'll often find yourself doing this anyway. Feel free to substitute words and images that are more meaningful and appropriate for you than those in the script.

Furthermore, don't hesitate to adapt or add to a suggested visualization in order to make it right for you. Add whatever objects, persons, symbols, or sensations "should be there"; change colors or descriptions to suit your needs. It's your imagination.

Additionally, if you like to think with your hands, to use gestures and physical motions, that's also perfectly acceptable in hypnosis. In fact, it is often very helpful to make the actual motions you'd make in the real situation being described. Actually hold the imaginary orange in your hand, scuff the imaginary floor with your real feet, make typing motions on your make-believe typewriter, or (what the heck) twirl your imaginary mustachios. If it helps you get the feelings of having a real experience, do whatever you'd like—as if you were a small child doing make-believe play.

If you understand these principles, and understand what it means to say that hypnosis is something you do, you have mastered this chapter. However, it's all been theoretical so far.

Let's do something practical—your first exercise. The exercises are generally longer than experiments and are meant to be done as homework, so to speak. Except as instructed, you will want to read a chapter, start practicing the exercises given in that chapter (most often at the end), and only then go on to read the next chapter. In the case of this first exercise, you can begin working on the next chapter immediately after doing it once or twice. While you work on the material in Chapter Two, you will be practicing the exercise on a daily basis.

Use your journal between experiments to keep track of unusual or interesting experiences, problems, insights, and any positive changes you observe from practicing your exercises. Your notebook will provide both a record of your progress and a very important means for mastering the material covered in this volume.

Exercise One: Progressive Relaxation With Suggestions

Purpose

To introduce one of the easiest-to-master and most effective techniques for deep mind-body relaxation, and to begin your exploration of working with your potentialities through hypnotic suggestion.

Method

Following taped instructions and guided fantasy.

Directions

Read through script to familiarize yourself with it. Then record yourself reading it aloud in a calm, clear, natural voice. Dramatize what you are saying and pause between stanzas or paragraphs, as appropriate. To practice once you have recorded the script onto a cassette, make yourself comfortable, reclining in a quiet room, and listen to your taped voice, doing or imagining as it directs. The exercise will take between 15 and 20 minutes. Practice at least once daily until you have done the exercise no less than five times before you go on to the experiments in Chapter Three.

Script

(For all taped sessions, leave 30 seconds of blank tape before you begin reading the first line).

"I am now going to relax more deeply than I have ever relaxed before.

"To begin, I will take a very deep breath and blow it out as slowly as I can. As I breathe out, I let myself go limp and loose. Here I go. . . . (Leave a 15-second pause before reading on, giving yourself time to breathe in.)

"Now I will tense my right foot and leg. I am squeezing all the muscles in my foot, bunching my toes, tensing my calf and thigh . . . bringing my leg up into the air as I tense and hold for a moment . . . hold . . . and now relax my right foot and leg, letting them drop back down gently as they relax. . .

"Now I tense my left foot and leg in the same way. I tense, squeeze . . . squeeze . . . relax . . . and they gently float back down and I can forget about my legs and feet. . . .

"I will now tense my right hand and arm. I make a ball of my fist and I squeeze . . . tensing my forearm . . . my upper arm . . . bringing the arm up into the air . . . I squeeze . . . squeeze . . . relax . . . and let my right hand and arm drift back down . . . loose and comfortable now. . . .

"And I squeeze my left hand and arm in the same way . . . I tense . . . tense . . . relax the muscles . . . and my arm and hand drift back down and relax. . . .

"Now I squeeze all the muscles of my butt and bottom . . . as if I were trying to stop peeing . . . I squeeze all the muscles of my pelvic floor . . . I can feel it . . . squeeze . . . my butt . . . my bottom . . . squeeze . . . relax. . . .

"And I tense all the muscles of my chest and back and tummy . . . I squeeze the muscles in my belly, my chest . . . I squeeze my shoulder blades together . . . tense . . . tense . . . and relax . . . I let all the muscles become limp and loose and comfortable and relaxed. . . .

"I now make a horrible ugly face, squeezing together all the muscles in my face, my jaw, my lips, my eyes, my forehead . . . I bring my head up a bit, tensing my neck . . . my scalp . . . I squeeze . . . squeeze . . . and relax. . . .

"Relax completely now . . . as I lie here relaxing, I feel myself breathing in and breathing out . . . as I breathe *in* I can feel as if I am sucking healing, cleansing, soothing and refreshing air in through my mouth and nose, down my windpipe into my lungs . . . soothing and relaxing them . . . and I can feel myself sucking this healing, cleansing breath of life in through my lungs into my bloodstream . . . turning my blood bright red with life and health . . . I feel this purifying fresh air flowing into every cell and organ and nerve and muscle of my body . . . soothing and relaxing every part of my body from my head to my toes . . . so good . . . it feels so good to just relax and let go and feel myself becoming more and more peaceful, calm, loose and limp and relaxed . . . so good. . . .

"As I breathe out, with every new breath I breathe out I can feel myself blowing out of my body and my mind all tightness, all tension . . . all ill health and discomfort . . . breathing myself calm and clear and fully relaxed . . . blowing every last little bit of tightness and tension and strain and stress and nervousness and anxiety out of my body and my mind . . . more and more with every new breath I breathe out . . . more and more calm and clear and pure and empty and more and more comfortably relaxed. . . .

"And I can just watch myself breathing in and blowing out at my own natural rate for a while . . . it feels so good . . . to drift and relax and let go and just *feel* myself breathing in and breathing out . . . so comfortable . . . so peaceful and calm and at ease . . . more and more so with every breath I breathe in and with every breath I breathe out for the rest of this session. . . ." (Leave the recorder running for 1 to 2 minutes now without saying a word.)

"So calm . . . so relaxed . . . so comfortable . . . it feels so good to just relax and drift along with my voice . . . so nice, so secure . . . so dreamy and peaceful . . . I let my mind drift and wander for a while . . . just floating until I feel as light as a cloud . . . a light, fluffy cloud lazily drifting in the clear blue sky of a spring afternoon . . . floating high above a lovely green valley . . . lazily, like a fluffy white cloud . . . feeling free and as high, as very peaceful, light, and comfortable as a cloud . . . .

"Far below I dream a green meadow . . . fragrant with soft green grass rippling softly in the warm afternoon breeze . . . birds singing in the trees by the side of this meadow . . . I can almost feel the fresh green leaves throbbing with growing life . . . reaching up, up, up toward the life-giving sun . . . full of life and health and joy . . . they raise their slender branches toward the warm afternoon sun . . . so alive. . . .

"And there's a merry little stream wandering through the meadow past the trees . . . clear, cool . . . pure as crystal . . . I can almost hear this little stream's voice as it lazily wanders through my meadow . . . clear and pure and cool and fresh . . . it would taste so lovely, so clean and pure and refreshing . . . a perfect stream with perfect green, cool, mossy banks . . . so soft and cool and mossy. . . .

"Like a cloud I drift across this meadow, high up in the pure clean air . . . floating across a spring afternoon . . . feeling the sun's bright rays slanting across the warm afternoon . . . the murmuring breeze . . . the gentle singing of birds . . . so perfect . . . so free . . . so completely at ease . . . I feel so cleansed . . . so relaxed . . . at peace . . . at peace with myself . . . at peace with the universe . . . so good . . . so good. . . ." (15-second pause)

"I feel ready to return to my everyday world now . . . as if I've been on vacation . . . I'm prepared to return to deal with the things of my life . . . knowing I can make it all work out . . . knowing I am okay . . . ready to face the things I have to do or deal with today and tomorrow . . . I'm okay . . . I can do it . . . it feels so good to be calm like this, knowing that it's okay . . . I can do it . . . I'm free . . . it feels so good to be free . . . to know that I'm okay . . . to really feel that I can do it . . . that I can relax and remain calm and enjoy my life and make things work out right for me . . . I have the power .. I can feel it . . . I'm free . . . I can feel the new energy, strength of mind and body within me now . . . growing stronger and stronger every new day . . . more and more alive and awake in my life . . . more and more calm, easy self-confidence, and aliveness inside myself . . . I can feel something wonderful happening . . . I'm ready now . . . I'm ready to *really* live . . . So I will take a deep, deep breath and while I'm breathing out I will count up from one to ten and then I will open my eyes and feel wonderfully awake, alert, alive, and completely refreshed . . . ready to really enjoy my life and make things work out right for myself . . . ready to face the rest of today and tomorrow in a new, calmer, more effective, more fully alive way . . . here I go: I will now breathe in, count up, and open my eyes . . ." (Leave 30 seconds of tape blank here, then say) "wide awake . . . wide, wide awake, feeling wonderful. . . ."

End of script. If you are at all concerned about falling asleep or missing appointments, set an alarm clock to go off 3 minutes after the end of your tape—once you have recorded it you'll know exactly how long it will be. When you have made your tape, rewind the cassette and just sit back and imagine along with your recorded voice. Keep the "how to" principles in mind and have fun. You will be amazed at what you can do and how good you can feel working with your tapes. Remember to keep a record of when you listen to your tapes and how it went for you in your notebook.

TWO

Yourself
Is Also Something
You Do

Strategic hypnosis is a method for using your thinking, feeling, and imagining to facilitate success in any or all aspects of your life. In order to obtain the things you want, however, it is essential to first understand what you are dealing with.

Only when you understand how things work can you work with them rather than against them. Therefore you need a way of analyzing that fits the facts. Even more important, you need a way of looking at things that facilitates doing something about them—you need a practically useful approach. When it comes to working with your own mental processes and your actual performance in everyday life, I believe you will find that the sociological form of social psychology, known as *symbolic interactionism*, fits the bill. In this chapter, we'll consider how this school of thought can be translated into your plan of action for self-improvement through strategic self-hypnosis.

Symbolic interactionism grew out of the pragmatist philosophy of William James and John Dewey. Its founder, the University of Chicago philosopher and social psychologist George Herbert Mead, began with the idea that human behavior differs from that of other organisms in a profound way.

Other animals react; humans act. Mead taught that people respond to situations and events in terms of the meanings things hold for us. Other creatures (so it was believed in the early decades of this century, at least) merely behave instinctually, in stimulus-response fashion. We humans, however, make our lives in a separate reality from the raw physical and biological environment; we never respond *directly* to the stimuli bombarding us.

We act on the basis of how we understand the situation to be. For example, you are walking down the street. A huge, hairy man in a sweatshirt stalks up to you. He socks you in the arm with his hamlike fist, a maniacal expression on his brutish face. What do you do?

At first you are, no doubt, shocked into paralysis. Then you notice his sweatshirt—why, it's from your alma mater, or your bowling team, or the local gym! You look at him again—it's old Harry! So you grin and say, "Well, you old S.O.B., how have you been?"

I'm sure something vaguely like that has happened to you at one time or another, although probably nothing so dramatic. The point is that you don't react to what happens, in and of itself; you search for and identify the cues that provide insight into the nature of the situation. Then you work out your response in terms of how you understand both what is happening and what the other person means by his or her actions.

There is something else peculiarly human about that encounter: symbolic interaction. Abstract meanings were exchanged through words, gestures, and other symbols, such as the design on Harry's sweatshirt. We can communicate ideas, information, hopes, and expectations. This allows us to cooperate. Isn't that better than fangs and claws?

The Self

Humans live in two realms. One is the shared social world, the other our own private experience. These two worlds are united; they intersect in the self.

This is something else peculiarly human. We are conscious of being ourselves; that is, we identify the answer to "Who and what am I?" in terms of a self-image or self-concept we have constructed in the course of growing up. We don't dream this up on our own. Rather, as we grow up in a world of other people, we learn to share their language, their life-style and culture and beliefs. We learn to see things "like a civilized person," and one of the things we learn to see is our self.

As we learn to join into the action around us, we begin to take the role, the part in the improvisational theater of life which others can accept as how we are. As we act the part, we come to identify with it, and to see ourselves as we believe others see us.

This is what I mean by the *self*; how I portray myself to me. It is that sense of *me*, of identity, of what *I* am in this world. My self-definition—it's how I plug myself into the world. At the same time, it plugs the world into my most private experience.

Don't get me wrong. I am personally enough of a mystic to accept the likelihood that at our core is something like a soul, a spirit, a transcendent aliveness. Certainly there is that phenomenon of awareness, of an "I" groping toward its world. *Cogito ergo sum* and all that.

Perhaps this is only a biological mirage, perhaps an intimation of God. In any case, it is not what I have been talking about. The self being described here is something you yourself have created in order to live in a shared human world.

There seems to be yet a deeper level of individuality beyond this, one not necessarily tied in any way to external social realities. We ought not take the pragmatist analysis *too* far, as humanistic psychology warns us.

Anyone reading this already has an essential self, an unshakeable sense of what is you. To ignore or repress or deny this level of your being is to cripple, frustrate, and ultimately block yourself from your true potentialities. It doesn't matter how you explain it. You've got your preferences, orientations, needs, your own ideas and feelings. The founder of humanistic psychology, Abraham Maslow, delved into this matter and came up with some good news: You can trust yourself, and by learning to express your own needs, preferences, motivations, and values you can make yourself not only the kind of person who can succeed in achieving his or her goals in life, but one who can live with and enjoy that fulfillment.

Still, in practice, we live very much in the reflections of reality we find in the eyes of others. I use the word *find* because, in truth, we cannot know what the other sees. We can only infer what goes on from their perspective. Comedy and tragedy alike can spring from this fact of our existence, so be aware and beware!

The Mind

This must be one of the most overused words in the English language.

Experiment Three: The Mind
Purpose
To see what we are talking about.
Method
Read and do. No need to tape—just use your notebook.
Directions
Define *mind.* I've been talking and talking about "your mind" and you've been reading along as if you knew what we were talking about. But do you really? Take a

minute or two to see if you can make clear to yourself just what we mean by *mind*. When you're done or when you give up, read on.

Near as I can gather, my mind is supposed to be an invisible organ of enormous power and capacity located within or somehow connected to my brain. Seriously, all the evidence we have indicates that there is no such thing as a mind. Your mind is, literally, a figure of speech.

But don't give up yet. Social psychologists don't deny the idea of mind—they build all their theories around it. However, they view mind as a series of acts, not a thing—as a process in which the organism pays attention to selected parts of its environment, interprets what is being noticed, and then builds up its line of response on the basis of that information. Mental processes allow you to construct your acts in the course of performing them, giving you one heck of an edge over preprogrammed robots.

In other words, you don't *have* a mind, you *do* your mind. The basic stuff of this mental process is your thinking.

In almost the same way you interact with other people, you maintain a conversation with yourself. I mean this literally. Mead called thinking the "I-me dialogue." Most social psychologists identity this with our background thinking or stream of consciousness. I find it useful to distinguish this internal exchange with one's self as *self-interaction*, labeling one's exchanges with the external world *hetero-interaction*.

Experiment Four: Listening to Yourself
Purpose

To see what all this theory is about for yourself.

Method

Introspection—just read and do, no need to tape.

Directions

Read through these instructions once and then just do as follows:

1. Close your eyes.
2. Take a few deep breaths to relax.
3. Now just listen to yourself thinking. Do you "hear" words? What are they saying? Is it one voice in particular or several voices?
4. Can you make your mind shut up? See if you can. (When you are ready, open your eyes and describe what you experienced or learned in your journal. Then read on.)

You were probably surprised by what a chatterbox your mind can be. (See, I'm using the term again—anything else is too clumsy, and besides, now you know what I mean.) Shutting up inside is quite an accomplishment in and of itself. It's so difficult, in fact, that Eastern cultures have developed all sorts of meditation practices for just that purpose. Don't be surprised if you couldn't do it on demand!

Recent studies have shed light on a second very important mental process—imagining. The eminent social psychologist and hypnosis researcher Theodore Sarbin considers imagining to be of central importance to the understanding of human behavior. He points out that this, too, is a process of symbolic self-interaction.

Little children specialize in make-believe play. They act out one fantasy after another—being Mommy cleaning house or Darth Vader zapping spacemen. Then, starting around the age we enter kindergarten, our parents, teachers, and peers all begin to drive home the message that "it's only your imagination," and that we must forsake such activities as we grow up. We do not, however, actually give up our fantasizing.

Rather, we learn to do it inside our heads. In what is known as imagining, daydreaming, or fantasy, we construct hypothetical situations and make-believe roles, visualizing how we would act in such and such a scenario. We merely learn to do this within our self-interactions rather than in the outside world.

Scientists are only now beginning to explore imagining. You're going to explore it quite thoroughly, however. It's the key to self-improvement.

The Definition of the Situation

It's not, you see, what really is but what you imagine to be that counts. This idea was first systematically explored in the years after World War I by the pioneering clinical sociologist W. I. Thomas. He conceptualized it as the *definition of the situation.* Paraphrasing Thomas, *what a person believes or takes for granted to be real is real in its consequences.*

The strategic method revolves around this. It's the key to miracles, or at least what might seem to be miracles.

Changing your life is a matter of changing your definitions of the situation. You must reconstruct your realities. By this term *reality*, we do not refer to whatever actually exists, but to your total sense of the big picture, your definition of *the* situation, your mental image of what really is, how and what things really are. It's all done with meanings—if you change what things mean for you, you change what they are for you.

Doesn't this sound like hypnosis? You let suggestions define reality and then act as if that definition of the situation was a simple statement of the facts. No matter how "unrealistic," screwy, naive, or perverse your definitions for the situation might seem to others, it is how you understand things to be that governs both what you can do and what you will do.

Foundations of Our Method

Symbolic interactionists recognize not only the conditioning influences of the social world upon the individual, but also the individual's autonomous power to act more or less freely within the constraints of his or her social and material situations. Radically unlike the psychiatric and behaviorist or conditioning theories dominating modern culture, this is a theory of liberty as opposed to determinism. Its message is that while we are social creatures, we are not only creatures of biology and environment, but creators also.

Our nature is not determined for us. Rather, as our biological parents contribute the raw material for our physical structure, our social world provides the raw stuff out of which we build our own lives and our selves. It is we who do the building.

How do we do that? By our *actions*. By our acts of thinking and imagining, we organize our conduct. We interpret and so define the situation for ourselves, and then we enact these ideas as conduct in the external world.

If we can change our definitions of the situation, we can change our performances in living. This is the loophole through which you can make yourself free, the foundation of the strategic method.

How do you change your inner realities? Through the same device by which you create and maintain them in the first place: through your self-interactions, your thinking, feeling, and imagining. By strategically guiding these mental processes, you can change both your inner reality and your outer act. Strategic self-interaction is the touchstone of our method.

For example, many of my hypnosis clients described themselves as compulsive overeaters. They had failed time and again to stick to a diet. So they'd tell me, "I try and try, but I just can't seem to stay off chocolates. No matter how hard I try to follow a diet, I always end up blowing it and going back to my old habits. I can't help it."

Clearly, this is a problem with their meanings. They have come to take for granted that chocolate, for example, is something that means so much for them they cannot resist it—it makes them feel better, it provides gratification, it helps them cope. Every time they have tried to deny these ideas, they create a hopeless double-bind situation in which they almost have to fail. It is like opening your eyes when you are making them stay closed. Therefore, in actual experience they have only confirmed the truth of that definition of the situation by their actions.

The approach I have normally taken with such cases illustrates what I mean by strategic hypnosis. Using their thinking and imagining, I help the "compulsive eater" redefine the meaning to themselves of food and eating. We work to develop an alternative definition of the situation, in which food is something they can take or leave as they choose, in which candy can be something they don't *need* and don't *have to want.* I find that redefinitions stressing one's liberty are vastly preferable to aversive tactics persuading the person that they can't eat the stuff or that it is horrid to them.

The strategic method, then, is applied symbolic interactionism. It is an example of the possibilities for effective therapeutic interventions which are now being realized by the rapidly expanding subdiscipline of clinical sociology.

The Structure of Self-Interaction

To master the logic of strategic self-hypnosis, you need to understand how your mind works. It is especially fruitful to look at human mental behavior in terms of two interlocking but distinct processes of self-interaction which we can call thinking and feeling. I will continue to use the term *mind* to refer to both of these lumped together or your mental behavior generally.

That human mental process is binary has long been suspected. However, the various theories about the mind make different sorts of distinctions and interpretations regarding the nature and meaning of thinking and feeling. Most familiar is the approach pioneered by Freud, in which we envision a vertical split between a conscious mind and the unconscious. Many popularized theories of hypnosis, for example, consider that it bypasses the conscious mind and works directly with the subconscious.

What I am presenting here in this volume involves an entirely different way of making sense of your mind. I am not dismissing nor slighting psychoanalytic thought in practice or theory—one cannot so easily ignore all the data pointing to unconscious processes. Rather, I am saying that a social behavioral analysis of the sort we are discussing in this chapter has greater practical relevance to what we are trying to do in strategic self-hypnosis. Being a pragmatist, I therefore adopt the model that best helps get the job done. So let's cut the theory and get to the meat. What are these two streams of self-interaction comprising your mind?

One I call thinking, for the obvious reason that it is what we normally mean by that term. Associated primarily with the activity of our brain's left cerebral hemisphere, thinking describes the verbal, logical, rational, and sequential acts manifesting in our self-talk, the internal "I-me" dialogue. This is the realm of the intellect.

As T. X. Barber reports, researchers have found that our background thinking goes on twenty-four hours a day. Apparently it is through this process of talking to ourselves, examined in Experiment Four, that we create and maintain our abstract, intellectual meanings for things. Within this stream of mental acts we think and plan out, solve puzzles, create imaginary scenarios and experiences, identify and make sense out of things. Thinking is the premier accomplishment of the human species.

However, it seems feasible to eventually develop an electronic computer that can duplicate thought. The idea of a world controlled by thinking computers has long been a theme of science fiction horror stories. Why is such a world so frightening and repugnant to us? Shall we investigate?

Experiment Five: Exploring Mental Processes
Purpose
To investigate for yourself the structure of mental process.
Method
Introspection guided by suggestion. Use your tape recorder for this one. As always, first familiarize yourself with the script and other directions, then tape yourself reading it, leaving 30 seconds blank before you begin speaking. Now listen to your tape, following along with your suggestions.
Script
"I now close my eyes and take a few deep breaths, relaxing myself so I can really concentrate.

"I am not going to think of something scary. I am not going to think of movies, stories, or scary experiences that send a chill up and down my spine. I am going to try and not think about the sorts of things that deliciously scared me as a child, a teenager, or an adult.

"I won't think about these things. I am going to ignore the pictures and words and ideas that flash through my mind when I think about them. I am not going to think about roller coasters and scary movies or horror houses or ghosts and goblins and things that make scary noises in the night." (Leave 60 seconds blank.)

"Now I can open my eyes and all the negative thoughts and feelings will vanish when I open my eyes and take my first few breaths in the safe, warm light." (Wait 30 seconds.) "I'm okay now. I feel great."

End of script. Consider now what differences there would have been had a computer and not yourself experienced these things. What is the difference between a thinking machine and a person thinking the same thoughts? Write your comments in your notebook and read on.

We're coming to a sphere of mental process that is difficult to speak of because we are seeking to describe not verbal but nonverbal, nonrational, sensual, intuitive acts of your entire organism. Your muscles, glands, and entire physical system are involved, shifting and flowing as your body echoes all the subtle activities appropriate to the actual situation or experience you are representing to yourself.

I'm trying to describe a sensual or sensorimotor definition of the situation which is literally frozen action, your body's image of how it would feel to actually be in that situation. It's not in words or thoughts, so you rarely notice it as something you are doing; you just *feel* the sensations appropriate to the situation, as when you imagined something scary.

It is fashionable to locate this mental process in your right cerebral hemisphere. Brain lateralization theories of this sort are, I am convinced, too limited in scope. The feeling process seems to be a kind of thinking with your whole body, not just one portion of your brain. It's a function of the entire organism—what I like to call a gut-level definition of the situation.

This form of thinking does not seem to be limited to humans, or to require so specialized a brain as ours. Rather, I believe that sensorimotor thinking is something beasts can do in varying degrees of refinement depending on the organization of their bodies.

Watch a dog, cat, or horse sometime. My cat lies napping in my study. His tail begins to twitch. His paws flex and retract. His eyes open and focus on something in the hallway. Suddenly his entire body ripples into action as he springs off the sofa and scoots out of the room. I am convinced that I have watched him "thinking" in cat fashion.

Similarly, I've watched sleeping dogs dream. I know that they aren't capable of intellectual thought, but they still seem to dream. I've watched dogs replay the motions of an entire episode. Sometimes they growl or whimper while deep asleep and dreaming. Observations like these convince me that mind should not be thought of as an entirely human domain. Or rather, that there is this other, more ancient form of mental process available to animals, involving one's entire organism as a sort of analog computer.

Apparently in the form of patterns of muscular tension, we symbolize and store in coded fashion our total organism's acts involved in experiencing and dealing with a situation. This serves, upon recall, to remind us of the meaning of the situation expressed in terms of the physical behaviors associated with it—how it literally feels. Thus, when you imagine a scary situation, you bring back the sensations associated with it, as in your last experiment.

Working With the Two Mental Processes

A sound analysis offers a prescription for practical action. The material in this chapter suggests our strategy for working with oneself.

Most people think of hypnosis only in terms of direct suggestions like "You will not eat chocolates." That, in reality, is a primitive technique of very limited application. However, it illustrates an entirely intellectual approach to personal change.

Body-oriented techniques have more recently come into vogue. Practitioners of bodywork use massage, role playing, and other tactics to release chronic patterns of tension. However valuable such techniques can be, they are not very relevant to our present needs or interests.

Unfortunately, the rediscovery of feeling by humanistic psychology has led to the claim that it is somehow better than intellectual thinking. Nonsense. If there are two parts to your mind, you are intended to use both. You come closest to operating at your full potential when you employ both of them in harmonious coordination. This is the royal road to maximum performance, the way of strategic self-hypnosis.

When acting rationally, we initiate conduct by intellectually defining a situation in terms of how we can classify it with regard to what we are already familiar with. Then, as we think about and name the object or event, we respond to our own thoughts by releasing the feelings we've associated with "that kind of thing." We're now *imagining* it. On the basis of this inner sense of what is really going on, we rationally work out our line of response.

However, much of the time we only become aware of what's going on in midstream, as we are already responding. What we notice about a situation, too, tends to precede our conscious thought. In these cases, we've begun by acting upon our nonrational, gut-level definition of the situation. In fact, routine and spontaneous conduct seem to bypass our intellectual guidance, as a rule. We find ourselves behaving as we know we should, as our bodies tell us. Feeling-level definitions of the situation, then, guide our habitual conduct.

At some point in the process of acting, the two streams of symbolic interactions come together. By bringing these together in the *imagining* process, we can construct the hypothetical situation in holistic fashion. The dimension of feeling lets us reinstate the sense of the whole, while intellectual meaning permits us to abstractly manipulate the possibilities in terms of structure, function, characteristics, or analogy to what we classify as similar situations.

Brought together in this way, the two streams generate what we might call a fantasy image. Like holograms—three-dimensional visual images produced by the interaction between two coded sources of light—this form of definition of the situation contains more information than is obtainable from either source alone. However, once we generate the image, we tend to respond to it as if it were the reality it symbolizes. We find ourselves unwittingly thinking and feeling in response to our own imaginations.

One important difference between the fantasy image and the "real world" is that we can imagine anything any way we'd like, whether or not such a thing actually exists. At the same time, fantasy images, our analogs of reality, can seem to us as real as life itself—more so, perhaps, because they are the only reality we can ever know completely.

You might see now the enormous power of your imagination. This therapeutic potential of fantasy images is already being exploited by a variety of counselors. One of the fathers of modern clinical hypnosis, William S. Kroger, M.D., has even come to advocate "imagery conditioning" as a primary tactic in all phases of psychotherapy. Our purposes are far more modest than Dr. Kroger's, but our approach is quite similar in practice.

In this volume, you'll be learning ways of developing hypnotic strategies by which you can construct specific fantasy images and episodes to indirectly get at your innermost mental processes. Through this approach you can directly or indirectly work with any or all of your hidden potentialities and program your spontaneous conduct. But to get what you want out of this self-hypnosis program, you need to have some idea of how your mind works and what it is that you are trying to do with your thinking, feeling, and imagining.

A Note on the Subconscious

Nearly as overworked as the concept of the mind is that of the subconscious. Time and again, popularizers of hypnosis have explained that it works directly with your subconscious. Many techniques of hypnotism are expressly designed to boggle your conscious mind and give the hypnotist direct access to this "other mind."

However, an increasing number of researchers have

come to question the assumption that those words actually refer to anything, just as we question the idea of a mind. Yet it is clearly mistaken to believe that your mental processes only consist of those acts and events you are aware of. Similarly, it is foolish to carry our definition-of-the-situation concept to the point of believing that only what you define as real can affect you.

In both cases, there is the problem of that which lies outside your personal consciousness. Clearly, most of what goes on in this universe falls into that category. Similarly, most of what you are doing within yourself is subconscious. I am speaking literally, using the term in its proper sense, as an adjective. There is no need to invent another mind within yourself.

Rather, we can follow the conclusions of the great turn-of-the-century psychologist and philosopher William James, that consciousness is not a *thing*, but something you do, the process of making yourself aware. We explored this approach with reference to your mind; Mead's social psychology is essentially a theory of human self-consciousness.

If we take this approach, it becomes apparent that you cannot be conscious of the acts by which you make yourself conscious. As you probably noticed in the experiments of this chapter, your mental activity proceeds most of the time on an automatic basis—you don't have to pay them any conscious attention at all.

That's what I mean by subconscious. In general, you are unaware of all the little routine actions you must go through in order to do or experience anything consciously. You just do them—once you have made something your routine, you can forget about it and just perform the sequence of acts habitually. This is the underlying nature and purpose of any habit.

For example, you have been reading this book (you're almost done with the most difficult section, by the way). Until this moment, have you been aware of the tiny motions of your eyes as you scan this page? Of what the rest of your body has been doing? Have you really noticed turning the pages? If I've written well enough to capture your attention, you'll have been aware of little else than the messages you are recreating in your mind. Once you've learned to read, the actions of reading become habitual and the process of going through these actions becomes subconscious.

Human Potentialities

I don't wish to mislead you. That of which you are conscious, even within yourself, is like the tip of an iceberg, the outermost sphere of a Chinese puzzle.

It is possible that beneath the finite masks of ourselves we are ultimately limitless in our true capacities. We may well be nearly godlike beings. I am inclined to suspect we fall something short of that, but our potentialities remain, at the very least, mind-boggling.

I don't know. I can only wonder about the true limits of my innate potentialities—and yours. I really don't know very much truth at all. There are things I believe and things I suspect and things I conclude and opinions I hold and dreams I have and will always dream—but none of these are the same as knowing. I don't know when I started and I can't really accept that I will end. Each day, however, I become more and more certain that Gautama Buddha was right—all these things are beside the point.

The best I can figure is that if I do my best here and now to live the kind of life I can feel good about, then the future and all matters spiritual and cosmic will take care of themselves in due course. The task before me is to live.

What, then, can we know about our potentialities? What do we have to work with?

Let's turn the question around. One thing is clear: Every choice you make, everything you do is a kind of cage. It is a cage because by being this or choosing that you can't be doing something else. Every action you take excludes a range of alternative possibilities.

While you can never know all your potentialities, you can become aware of some of your own limits. By recognizing and understanding the cages you have built for and around yourself, you can begin to do something about those you've come to find too restricting.

Some of the hardest barriers to overcome are those imposed upon us by language, culture, and our location in history and society. My Jewish ancestors had few choices open to them in medieval Europe. They couldn't be doctors, they couldn't be kings, but they were allowed to become tradesmen.

Other cages are more personal, although they too reflect one's social world. Take our selves—growing up in America, we learn what everybody takes for granted we can do, will do, won't do, and can't do. Why would I even bother to try levitating or blowing your nose? More seriously, much of what we learn about ourselves in the course of growing up and constructing our self-definition is negative. We learn what we are not, what we can't do, or what a person "like ourselves" wouldn't choose to do even if he or she could.

You're not smart enough for this, strong enough for that, pretty enough or handsome enough for the other. Boys don't cry and girls don't do better than boys at math. Slum kids don't hope to become poets and scientists, upper-middle-class kids don't learn how to handle knives.

We also learn more subtle ways of encaging ourselves, of blocking ourselves from our own potentials. Until recently, who would have believed that some women can make their breasts larger by suggestion, or that someone like yourself could very likely lower his or her blood pressure by spending a few minutes a day with his or her eyes closed mumbling "anything" over and over again? It was generally known to be a scientific fact that you can't do anything about such bodily processes.

I've chosen each of these examples to show you how wrong one's beliefs about reality can be. You don't know what you could do. But instead, you let yourself be guided by false ideas telling you that you mustn't even try the walls of your cage. You must adjust to "the realities of life" and forget your dreams.

This is a book about adjusting the realities of life to achieve your fullest potentials. *What could you be or do or have if only you knew it were possible, if only you knew a way of going about attaining those things, and if you could allow yourself to do so?*

That's what this book is really about. Strategic self-hypnosis is but a means for accomplishing those things. There is no magic in these techniques—the magic and the power are your own. To unfold your true potentialities, you must do two things. First, you must cease blocking yourself off from your own abilities, you must cease acting in such a way as to keep yourself a victim of life and of the people and situations around you. Second, you must develop some new strategies and tactics for successful living and you must use them. That's the bottom line. You've got to act.

But the keystone, the cornerstone, and the foundation of our method lie within your grasp. You can change your ideas, redefine what is "only real" for yourself; and by strategically using your own thinking, feeling, and imagining, you can take charge over your life and make it work out right for you—as you yourself choose to judge such things.

There are no known limits upon what you might accomplish through strategic self-hypnosis. The only limitations are those you impose upon yourself (which may or may not be the same as those you'll find you can't overcome no matter how long or how hard you strive).

You have begun an adventure, a journey into an unexplored land—yourself.

However, even while nobody can know what you'll find, you need at least a preliminary map or plan of action. You've got to start somewhere. It's best to begin at the most practical level—and what's more practical or important than overcoming your problems, unwanted habits, or other things you wish to change about yourself or your "act"? The following exercise should help you sort things out and begin your journey toward self-mastery. Before you're done with this book, you'll probably want to revise your initial goals and approaches. However, to begin, why not take an hour or so and do something very worthwhile for yourself?

Exercise Two: Self-Assessment
Purpose
> To sort out what's going on in your life and develop your initial plan of action.

Method
> Pen-and-paper exercise (use your notebook or scrap paper when working on it, then write down your list or lists in your notebook for future reference).

Directions
> As follow. You might want to make two separate lists. The first list should itemize those things you feel keep you from being okay in your own eyes (for some of these you may choose to work with a counselor or other professional). Your second list should concern going beyond merely okay to maximum performance and exploring your fullest potentialities.
>
> 1. Make a list of answers to the question "What's bugging me?" Write down anything you aren't happy or satisfied with in your life, anything that is a problem for you. Consider your self, your body, your feelings, your relationships, your behaviors, your work, or your performance in any other area of your life. Be specific, describing each item in concrete detail rather than just writing down a name for what you are thinking about.
> 2. Number these items in order of their importance or urgency for you—let number one be the most important, number two the second most important to resolve, etc.

3. Now make a second list. For each of the items on your first list, in order, write down how you would rather behave or feel or be. That is, write down your goals with respect to each item on your "what's bugging me" list. Again, make your list descriptive, spelling out what you're talking about.

4. At this point, you might want to review your priorities in light of your goals. Renumber your items, if appropriate.

5. Go back to your "what's bugging me" list. What part of each item seems to be *built in?* (E.g., being a nurse is inherently stressful; stress comes with the job.) What part of each item seems to boil down to what *other people are doing?* (E.g., an alcoholic spouse creates problems for you.) Third, what part of each item seems to be the result of what *you are doing, not doing, or how you are reacting?*

6. For each item on your "what's bugging me" list, write down what you are doing to keep the situation stuck as a problem to you. Not what you mean to do or are trying to do, but as you have asked yourself in step 5, how you act or react so as to perpetuate the problem or make it affect you negatively. If there are more than five items on your list, see if you can group them into no more than five related bunches, or else do only steps 6 through 9 for the five most important items in your own priorities.

7. Now consider, for each of your five items, what you feel you could realistically do in order to change the situation and make it better for you.

8. Transfer your list of "what's bugging me" to your notebook. List each problem area, how you want it to be instead, and what you can do (or stop doing) so as to resolve or change that situation in the direction of your goals for yourself.

9. You are now ready to begin doing something about

it. Starting off with item number one, if you have determined that there is something you can do about it, begin. If it is a problem of learning how to do something or how to do it better, and such training is available to you, set about getting that help. Self-hypnosis will primarily serve for relaxation, reinforcement, and as a learning device. If, on the other hand, the item necessitates redefining your limits, acquiring new self-control skills, or changing how you act or react in problem situations, then the self-hypnosis will provide a direct training and self-help function.

You can go on to the next chapter while you are working on your self-assessment, although it's better to first complete it and then go on.

Note: In any case, if you feel the problems are very deep or extremely frustrating, or if you cannot get anywhere on your own, you should consult a clinical psychologist, sociologist, psychiatrist, or other counselor. If there are medical problems (if you want to lose weight), first consult a physician or other health-care professional. If the problem is not one that seems to require therapy, you might wish to consult a professional hypnotechnician.

THREE

What Do You Do When You Do Hypnosis?

In this chapter we will complete our discussion of hypnosis itself. The remainder of this volume will be devoted to the strategic applications of hypnosis in your actual everyday life. First, though, it is necessary to consider what it means to "do hypnosis."

There are many theories of hypnosis which have been proposed by researchers and clinicians over the years. A few of these are downright wrong. For example, there is no longer any question that hypnosis is not a matter of animal magnetism or a mysterious power emanating from the hypnotist's eyes. You'll still see it portrayed that way in some books and old movies, but that theory's long dead. Neither is hypnosis a matter of a stronger will overriding a weaker will; being "suggestible" is not a mark of weakness nor personal pathology. Yet traces of this theory, too, persist in the popular consciousness.

There is, however, no single theory about hypnosis accepted by the scientific community as a whole. Currently dominating the field is a family of theories explaining hypnosis in terms of an altered state of consciousness known as hypnotic trance.

Explanations of this type hold that hypnotic induction

procedures enable subjects to dramatically shift mental gears and enter the hypnotic state. The ability to do so, many feel, is an individually variable trait known as suggestibility or hypnotic susceptibility. The highly suggestible individual can, under the proper conditions, enter a deep hypnotic state in which that person can be guided to do things not possible in normal waking consciousness.

The leading proponent of this school of thought is probably Dr. Ernest Hilgard. From his findings at the Stanford University Laboratory of Hypnosis Research, Professor Hilgard has generalized seven basic characteristics of this hypnotic state:

1. The subject becomes relatively passive, letting the hypnotist's suggestions define and control his or her conduct and experience.
2. The process of selective attention becomes pliable, so that suggestions can cause to notice or not notice parts of the actual environment as the hypnotist directs.
3. There is a marked enhancement in the subject's ability to recall and create sensory memories, images, or entire fantasy episodes.
4. The subject ceases to pay much attention to considerations of reality, becoming more able to uncritically accept suggestions—however bizarre—as "the real thing."
5. The subject becomes more suggestible; that is, more willing and able to respond as if involuntarily to suggestions.
6. Similarly, he or she tends to automatically adopt and enact roles suggested by the hypnotist.
7. Very commonly, the subject exhibits amnesia for what transpired while hypnotized.

Hilgard and other researchers, many of whom were his students, have also identified what amounts to an eighth characteristic:

8. Subjects report that they experienced a dramatically altered state of consciousness accompanied by qualitative changes in their thinking, feeling, or perceiving while in hypnosis.

All the controversy surrounding the nature of hypnosis—and this is one of the hottest issues in psychology—revolves around how to make sense of these characteristics. Even among theories describing hypnosis as an altered state, explanations range from a psychoanalytic model of hypnosis as ego regression to cybernetic models likening hypnosis to reprogramming a computer. Most clinicians seem to accept the idea that hypnosis is some kind of altered state.

However, two of the most respected researchers in this area, Theodore Sarbin and T. X. Barber, have seriously questioned the validity as well as the value of interpreting hypnotic phenomena as evidence of a special hypnotic state. Rather, they argue, everything that has been observed with regard to hypnosis can be explained in terms of normal mental processes.

For these researchers, hypnosis is something you can do—a special way of using your mind. They argue that it is all done by your acts of thinking, feeling, and imagining, so there is no need to invoke something as extraordinary as an altered state of consciousness to explain the "mysteries of hypnosis."

Would you like to investigate for yourself?

Experiment Six: What Is Hypnosis Like?
Purpose

To experience for yourself a conventional hypnosis session.

Method

Imagining along with your recorded voice, exactly as in previous experiments.

Directions

For this and all other experiments and exercises using hypnosis or visualization, it is essential to follow four rules:

1. Practice in a comfortable place free from intrusions, loud or sudden noises, or other distractions. Dim the lights, turn off the TV or stereo, close the door, ask to be left alone for a while except for real emergencies, turn off the telephone if you can, etc.

2. Make yourself physically comfortable. It is best to rest in a recliner or soft chair that supports your neck, head, and back. You might prefer to prop yourself up on a bed or sofa (but avoid lying flat). Find a position in which you can be comfortable for a half hour or more, one in which you can relax completely. Loosen or remove tight clothing, take off eyeglasses, remove any gum from your mouth, and— very important!—take out contact lenses.

3. Leave at least 30 seconds blank at the start of your tape so you will be able to get into position and become comfortable. Leave at least 30 seconds blank after the end of your script and then, perhaps, say in a loud voice, "Wide, wide awake . . . feeling wonderful." You might also set an alarm to go off a few minutes after your tape will end. Don't practice when you are very tired, or you may well go to sleep (unless, of course, you want to go to sleep).

4. Most important of all, cooperate with yourself to the very best of your ability. Act like a good subject. Let things flow. Expect to have an enjoyable and beneficial time and you will do so. *Hypnosis is a form of play*—keep that in mind and you can't go wrong!

Script

"To begin, I am going to look up with my eyes and find a spot on the ceiling somewhere above the center of my hairline. I am going to focus my attention on that spot with all my might and keep staring at the spot for as long as I can.

"As I stare at my spot, I will take a deep breath and hold it for as long as I can and then breathe out slowly, as slowly as I can, and as I breathe out I let my body go limp and loose and relaxed . . . I breathe in starting *now,* even as I keep on staring at that spot on the ceiling . . . And I'll keep on staring at that spot while I breathe out, letting nothing distract me . . . and I'll keep staring at that spot as I begin breathing in and breathing out naturally, automatically . . . more and more slowly as I begin to relax. . . .

"I'll keep staring at that spot as I breathe in and breathe out and I can feel my body starting to let go and feel limp and loose and relaxed . . . my knees feel heavy now . . . heavier and heavier . . . as I stare at my spot on the ceiling I can feel this heaviness spreading down through my knees . . . from my knees down through my feet to my toes . . . and my toes relax and feel heavier and staring at that spot becomes harder and harder for me as my eyes begin to water and they want to blink more and more . . . my legs feel heavier and heavier with every downward blink of my eyelids . . . I feel more and more relaxed . . . drowsier . . . dreamier . . . with every breath I breathe in and breathe out . . . my eyes feel dreamier and driftier and drowsier and more and more relaxed. . . .

"Eyes want to close now . . . but I won't let them close for as long as I can keep them from closing . . . the pleasantly heavy numbness is spreading up through my body now . . . so nice . . . so dreamy and peaceful and drowsy and warm . . . so nice . . . so hard to keep staring . . . the harder I try the more I relax . . . the spot . . . relaxes me . . . too hard to keep staring much longer . . . eyes just want to relax . . . my lids feel so heavy now

. . . every breath I breathe in and every breath I breathe out . . . I feel more and more dreamy, sleepy, slow, and relaxed . . . breathing more and more slowly now . . . slow and regular . . . deep and slow . . . drowsy and sleepy . . . drifting and drifting . . . more and more. . . .

"Sleepier and dreamier every breath I breathe out . . . the strain in my eyes is growing heavier and heavier and it's just a matter of time before they close by themselves . . . eyes are so tired . . . so tired . . . drowsier and drowsier with every breath I breathe in . . . the dangers of hypnosis are a myth . . . this is fun . . . it's like being a child again and having fun . . . make-believe fun . . . my eyes may be closing now or they may be already closed . . . now . . . I feel so drowsy and happy as I listen to my voice and drift with my voice now . . . making believe I'm deep asleep and just dreaming everything I hear myself say . . . soon I will really feel deep asleep . . . but I'll still hear and respond to everything I say on this tape or in any session of hypnosis and I can always bring myself back to full, wide-awake consciousness by just taking a deep breath and counting up to ten . . . I know I can do that and I'll always remember that I can do it whenever I need to . . . breathing in deeper and deeper . . . and I'll always notice anything that happens around me that really needs my attention . . . so I can relax . . . I can trust myself . . . but now I want to go deeper . . . as I breathe out . . . if my eyes are not quite closed I'll close them now and let them relax. . . .

"Relaxing more and more now . . . I can let myself relax and really feel what hypnosis can be like for me . . . I am ready now . . . ready to go all the way into hypnosis . . . drifting now . . . more and more . . . drowsy and relaxed . . . dreamy and sleepy . . . very, very sleepy now . . . I can feel something happening . . . very, very pleasant . . . very, very safe . . . it feels so good

. . . here I go . . . all the way down . . . into real deep hypnosis . . . deep into myself . . . I will count down from ten to one very slowly and by the time I'm all the way down to one I'll be more deeply relaxed and dreamy than I have ever been before . . . and after one I'll go down to zero . . . and when I say zero I'll let myself feel as if I were deep asleep and dreaming . . . dreaming I respond to every suggestion I can hear my voice say . . . easily and automatically . . . because I want to . . . here I go, all the way down . . . ten [10-second pause] . . . nine, deeper [9-second pause] . . . eight, drifting more and more now [8-second pause] . . . seven, all the way down [7-second pause] . . . six [6-second pause] . . . five, sleepier and sleepier [5-second pause] . . . four [4-second pause] . . . three, feeling deep now [3-second pause] . . . two, deep asleep [2-second pause] . . . one, one, one [10-second pause] . . . zero . . . zero . . . zero . . . zeeerowwww . . . deeper and deeper with every breath I breathe in for the rest of this session . . . dreamier and sleepier with every breath I breathe out for the rest of this experiment. . . ." (Leave 3 minutes of silence here.)

"Now I am fixing in my mind exactly how I am feeling . . . when I wake myself up after this experiment, I will very clearly remember exactly how I feel at this moment . . . right after the *induction*. . . .

"Now as I relax more and more completely, I can feel like a small child on a wonderful holiday outing . . . and I will remember a helium balloon . . . perhaps one I may have had as a very small child . . . I can imagine my balloon now . . . it's a magical color . . . a magic balloon . . . I clutch the string to my balloon in my little hand now . . . I make believe my balloon is in my hand now and I can really feel it . . . more and more. . . .

"I peek at the hand in my mind's eye . . . it's so

small and tiny . . . delicate . . . childlike . . . and I watch the balloon this hand of mine is holding . . . my very own balloon . . . so pretty . . . it makes me think of birthday parties and circuses and parades and wonderful good times . . . and see, the number *zero* is printed on my balloon . . . like the outline of an egg . . . I can see it so clearly . . . what color is that zero? . . . I'm going to hold onto my balloon for a little while longer and for as long as I hold onto my balloon I'm gonna watch the zero and make sure it doesn't change colors or go away . . . it's my balloon. . . .

"This is so much fun . . . it's so easy and natural for me to work with hypnosis . . . every time I do hypnosis or self-hypnosis it comes easier for me, and as I concentrate on my zero I feel more and more as if this were all a wonderful happy dream . . . a dream of my very own . . . and I know now I can make hypnosis work for me . . . I feel it . . . and I keep on watching my balloon and feel it tugging ever so gently on my hand. . . .

"With every breath I breathe in I seem to be blowing up my magical balloon with more and more magical floating balloon gas . . . and my balloon seems bigger and rounder and lighter and lighter and I float deeper and deeper and soon I'm going to count out loud backward from three down to one, and when I hear myself say 'one' I'm going to just let the balloon gently, gently tug my hand and arm up, up a few inches into the air . . . and my arm will want to float there all by itself . . . I will not raise my arm too rapidly . . . I'll just let it happen . . . I'll be like an innocent bystander and just watch what happens . . . but I'll start whispering 'zero' to myself and keep on saying 'zero' in my mind as I watch my wonderful magical balloon . . . and every time I think 'zero' it will become lighter and floatier and before I realize it my arm will float a few more inches up high into the air . . . because I am blowing my balloon up so light and floaty . . . the more I relax and watch and think 'zero' the balloon becomes more and more lighter still and my hand keeps drifting up and up and up into the air . . . I can actually feel my magical balloon pulling it up ever so slowly . . . until it floats straight up all the way into the air as high as my hand can go . . . here I go:

"Three [3-second pause] . . . two [2-second pause] . . . one, one, one . . . my arm is gently floating . . . lifting . . . up . . . and up and up . . . drifting into the air and it hangs there for a while becoming still lighter and it wants to drift higher into the air and I drift deeper and float more and more into dreamy, peaceful hypnosis as my breathing becomes slower and deeper and more regular and my arm wants to lift higher and higher into the air . . . so I say zero . . . zero . . . zero . . ." (On your tape, keep on saying "zero" for one minute, pausing slightly longer between each "zero," and then say "zero" for another 15 to 30 seconds at a normal talking speed.)

"In a few moments I am going to open my eyes and when I do I will be able to see and feel exactly what my hands and arms have been doing with themselves . . . first, I am fixing into my mind how I am feeling right now, at this moment, so I can remember exactly how I felt after this experiment is over . . . I will remember everything I experienced during this session . . . I will remember everything I felt and thought in this session 45 seconds after I count up to ten . . . but not until those 45 seconds have gone by . . . this first time I open my eyes I can do so and remain deeply relaxed . . . I open my eyes right *now.*

"As I watch with my eyes open, I will say 'zero' one more time and when I say 'zero' I will open my hand and let go of my balloon and watch it float away out of sight into the sky and my hand and arm will feel normal and comfortable once again and I will once

again feel like a grown-up.... Here goes: zero! ...
good-bye balloon ... I'm closing my eyes and going
deeper now ... and I tell myself that when I open my
eyes again in a few moments I am going to feel great ...
relaxed ... refreshed ... rejuvenated ... really alive ...
feeling really sure of myself and my ability to master
self-hypnosis and accomplish my goals ... nothing can
stop me now ... but for exactly 45 seconds after I next
open my eyes, I may feel as if I cannot remember a
thing that has happened to me from the time I counted
down to the number five ... this may puzzle me ...
then, when the 45 seconds have passed, I will clearly
remember everything in vivid detail ... okay ... I am
ready to begin to really live ... starting now ... one,
two, three, four, five, six, seven, eight, wide awake
now, nine, really feeling great, ten ... I open my eyes
... [pause 50 seconds] ... really feeling great now ...
positively wonderful ... wide, wide awake!"

(End of script. Make notes in your journal regarding (a) What happened, what did you experience?
(b) Were you really asleep? (c) Was it really hypnosis?
(d) How would you describe what was going on? *Save
your tape for use in Exercise Five at the end of this
chapter.*)

A Pragmatic Approach

Let me explain to you what I've concluded about
hypnosis. This pragmatic approach incorporates insights
from all major scientific theories, but relies most heavily
upon the viewpoints of Sarbin and Barber. As you would
expect, I start out from the sociological perspective discussed in our last chapter. My goal is to provide a useful
way of looking at hypnotic phenomena, something that can
guide you in your practical application of self-hypnosis to
your own life.

We begin by observing that the term "hypnosis" is

used in two different ways. We use this word to describe the *social situation* within which "hypnosis" takes place, but also to describe the "hypnotized" subject's *frame of mind*.

The social situation is of a very special kind, quite unlike a normal conversation with a friend or acquaintance. It is marked by *intensive* and *purposeful* social interaction. Communications are all directed toward achieving specific goals; everything about what is being said has a purpose. Even more importantly, the initial exchanges are directed toward fully absorbing the subject's attention in the flow of talk.

This sense of intensiveness is most important. Hypnotic performances are made possible (at least in large part) by the fact that the more involved you become in your interactions with another, the fuzzier and more vague becomes the rest of the world for you—until all other realities become almost entirely excluded from your awareness. You see this occurring in situations such as evangelical meetings, passionate conversation between lovers, or getting absorbed in a good movie.

In the hypnotic situation, this absorption is deliberately built up to an extraordinary degree. Before starting, we act to minimize any distractions (as in notes 1 and 2 in the above experiment). Then you are asked to focus on the hypnotist's voice, which proceeds to bombard you with a stream of suggestions.

At one level, these communications are designed to define the situation in a certain way. As the subject, your role is to more or less passively accept what is being transmitted to you. Almost like a television set, the subject is expected to merely assemble the information being communicated into make-believe performances in the theater of his imagination. There is, usually, no give-and-take. The hypnotist runs the show as a sort of scriptwriter, prompter, and director rolled into one. A good subject thinks, feels, imagines, or otherwise responds only as directed.

At the same time, the subject is being more subtly directed to pay attention only to the information being communicated to him or her by the hypnotist. The subject is to let this become the only reality, to act, at least, as if this were the only information there is.

Specific form is given to the actual session by the hypnotist's selection of words, images, and tactics. For example, the meaning of hypnosis is defined for you by what the hypnotist is saying and how he or she says it. It was once the general rule to speak in a monotonous, "hypnotic" voice, and to use a sleep wording, as in our experiment. These tactics were designed both to invoke the idea that the hypnotist alone controls the action and to further promote the passivity of the subject, as if that person were actually asleep and dreaming.

These directions almost always go on to imply that because—and only because—he or she has been hypnotized, the subject will do and experience things that would be difficult, unlikely, or inimaginable outside of hypnosis. This expectancy for unusual and ordinarily improbable things to occur is a hallmark of the hypnosis situation.

In structuring the situation, the suggestions are also directed toward facilitating the subject's adoption of a hypnotic frame of mind. It is not necessary to accept the idea of an altered state of consciousness to recognize that doing hypnosis successfully requires the subject to shift into a literally *extraordinary frame of mind.* While ordinarily we direct our mental processes toward coping with the outer world as we reconstruct or define it within our self-interactions, in hypnosis you shift your attention away from the objective universe, to focus instead upon the imaginary universes you construct internally. You literally forget about the "real world" and concentrate upon the ever-shifting inner reality you are creating for yourself as you think, feel, and imagine along with the suggestions.

This state or frame of mind is very much like that of a small child engaged in make-believe play or that of a person stoned on marijuana. Unlike those situations, however, that of hypnosis is deliberately and strategically structured, as I have discussed.

It works rather like this. I am the hypnotist, so I say some words to you: "Feel yourself relaxing." You are listening to me with all your might, and you hear these words I directed at you. Without conscious attention or effort, you translate what you heard into words and feelings defining the situation for you internally. As you do that, several things happen.

As you recreate my meanings for yourself, you generate and simultaneously experience a *fantasy image*, an internal analog or mock-up of reality based upon my suggestions. When I ask you to *think, feel,* or *imagine,* or to *see, picture,* or *tell yourself,* what I am really doing is coaxing you into constructing an imaginary experience. In daily life, you automatically construct images of this sort in the course of organizing your behavior within the framework of your preexisting realities. However, in hypnosis you normally create these definitions of the situation in order to reprogram your future conduct by changing those realities you take for granted.

As you do this, you cannot help but respond to what you are only imagining as if you were not experiencing a fantasy image but the real thing. Your body responds to your imagining in daily life, but relatively weakly. But when you are really absorbed, in a hypnotic frame of mind, you may find yourself spontaneously responding almost exactly as if what was suggested is actually occurring. You can get the same effect by imagining along with the suggestions *as if you were hypnotized,* by adopting that same frame of mind:

Experiment Seven: Responding to Fantasy Images
Purpose

 To investigate what can happen when you think, feel, and imagine along with suggestions.

Method

Imagining along with your recorded voice. For this particular exercise, you'll want to sit upright.

Script

"Sitting upright, I will place both of my hands straight out in front of me, with the palms facing down. As I do so right now, I make sure my hands are at the same level. Then I close my eyes.

"I tell myself that five very light, very floaty balloons are being tied, one onto each finger of my right hand. These helium-filled balloons are so light, so buoyant, they pull and tug my right hand up, up . . . up into the air, all by themselves. I tell myself I can feel these balloons, I can *feel* the lightness . . . I visualize these balloons and imagine that my hand wants to float up into the air because I can feel the pull of these five balloons . . . I can keep on thinking about and feeling these balloons pulling my hand up into the air . . . as if more and more helium balloons were being tied onto my right hand now . . . more and more balloons tugging my right hand higher and higher into the air with a stronger and stronger pull. . . .

"And while this is going on, I can also imagine a big, gray concrete block being lowered very carefully onto the top of my *left* hand . . . I can feel the heavy cinder block pressing itself down onto my left hand . . . it is very heavy . . . so heavy I can feel it now . . . more and more . . . I can imagine feeling the rough bottom of this heavy concrete block pressing down on my left hand . . . my skin feels that rough, heavy texture as its weight pushes down on my left hand . . . it's so hard to resist . . . the more I try to hold my left hand up, the heavier it gets . . . it grows heavier and heavier . . . as if another block is being piled on top of the first concrete block pressing down on my hand . . . I can feel the balloons tugging up on my right hand now and the heavy concrete blocks pressing my left hand down more and more . . . I really let myself imagine how it feels. . . .

"Now, without moving either of my two hands and arms, I will open my eyes and look at my hands and see what they have been doing while I've been imagining. Once I've done that, I can just relax both hands and arms and my entire body feels comfortable and normal again."

End of script. Once again, jot down some notes regarding what you felt during the experiment and what you observed at its end.

This experiment was designed to let you see your own psychosomatic responses to acts of thinking, feeling, and imagining. These are, as you will have noticed, subliminal and automatic. They occur regardless of whether or not you are aware of them. In effect, they represent your definition of the situation at the feeling level—you go through the motions of the actual experience you are only imagining, normally with but a ghost or representation to yourself of the full-blown response. However, when you really concentrate on the fantasy image, you can deliberately bring out stronger psychosomatic responses—as you have just learned.

The fact that you can respond to your definitions of the situation and fantasy images without feeling or being aware of what you are doing can lead to some problems. You can unwittingly trigger undesirable psychosomatic responses. You can also mislead yourself to confuse subconscious responses with manifestations of a hidden subconscious mind that is somehow more aware of what is really going on than you can ever be.

Here, for example, is a fun exercise in suggestion that has been used to "demonstrate" the existence of your subconscious, to tell the sex of unborn babies, and all sorts of other far-out things.

Experiment Eight: Cheveul's Pendulum

Purpose

To explore how you can deliberately shape subconscious psychosomatic response.

Method

Read and do, no need to tape. However, you'll need a pendulum. To make one, take a one-foot length of string (coat-and-button thread works great) and tie it to a shiny metal key or ring.

Directions

Sitting upright, hold the loose end of your string between thumb and forefinger, letting the pendulum hang down.

To begin, stop the motion of the pendulum with your free hand. Now, watching your key or ring, begin concentrating on the idea that it wants to move in a circular, counterclockwise direction. Keep watching as you tell yourself over and over that it is beginning to move in a counterclockwise circle. If you really concentrate on the idea that this is happening, you'll see the pendulum start to move around and around in a circle. Now see how fast you can make it go: Just tell yourself it is speeding up, moving faster and faster. It will. Don't move your hand; let your thoughts move the pendulum.

When you've done that, you can change the direction of your pendulum's motion in the same way. Just *picture* the ring or key moving in the opposite—clockwise—direction. Concentrate this time on visualizing it doing so; it may take a few moments to counter the momentum of your pendulum, but you'll soon get it circling around and around in this other direction. You can also try other motions—back and forth, etc. Just let yourself imagine the pendulum moving as you'd like.

You can vary what you are doing in another way, as well. Imagine something happening *that would cause the pendulum to do as you wish.* Be realistic at first—for example, imagine that as you breathe in, you are sucking the key or ring toward you, and as you breathe out, you are blowing it away from you. Work with this for a few moments and you'll find it an easy way to control the movement of your pendulum.

However, there is no reason why you have to imagine something realistic. Just so long as *what you are imagining, if it were true, would cause the desired effect*, it will work for you. Why not imagine that a tiny leprechaun or maybe a two-inch-high Mickey Mouse figure is running behind your pendulum pushing it in a circle with his tiny hands? It might help to close your eyes to get into the make-believe, but then you can open them once again and pretend you can see it actually happening. You may find this is the easiest way to control the pendulum. When you get tired of playing with your pendulum, you can stop. Make some notes for yourself regarding what worked best for you. Now when your friends say, "Oh, you're learning self-hypnosis—can you do it to me?" you can look smug and say, "Let me show you what I've learned." Have your friend hold the pendulum and, as you did with yourself, suggest how it will move. The usual response is "I didn't believe it was going to work!"

The Cheveul pendulum is an amusing way of observing your subconscious psychosomatic responses to your own thinking and imagining, even where there is nothing you can feel going on. The way it works is that your thinking and imagining triggers imperceptible muscular movements duplicating, however faintly, the actual motions you would experience if what you were visualizing were really going on. The mechanical device of the pendulum amplifies these tiny subliminal motions into something noticeable.

The pendulum can, in fact, be used in hypnosis as a

nonverbal signaling device. It is most often used by therapists to obtain repressed or long-forgotten information or to
overcome a subject's inability or resistance to communicate
something directly. In strategic self-hypnosis you won't be
working with that sort of problem, although you may wish
to experiment with a system (back and forth for yes, side to
side for no, etc.) allowing you to probe for hidden memories
or forgotten material.

The Skill of Doing Hypnosis

In the guise of lecturing at you, I have been training
you in the skill of doing hypnosis. You know what to do
now: Relax, let go, and allow yourself to wholeheartedly
think, feel, and imagine along as if you were actually experiencing those things being suggested. You know that you
can't do this by brute force or effort, only by following the
rules every child knows for make-believe play.

You start the process off self-consciously by pretend-
ing it's already happening, thinking yourself into feeling as
if—for example—you were actually holding a balloon you
can see. Before long, however, you seem to be on the
outside, watching the experience unfold itself. It's no longer
as if you are doing it—it takes on all the qualities of an
objective reality. When that happens, you know you are
doing hypnosis right.

We are all different, however. Each of us will find
our own best way of working hypnotically. You will experience your hypnosis in your own way—so don't worry
about it.

One thing many people do worry about is whether
they know how to imagine. Sometimes they tell me, "I have
no imagination." Other people are worried that their fantasy images are too vague, or that they cannot "*see* it in their
mind" (although they "kind of know it's there").

Once again, people are all different. Some are good
at visualizing in pictures, others at feeling, still others at

hearing or in some other way sensing what they are imagining. A few of us have to, at first, tell ourselves that we are experiencing it and take it on faith. It doesn't matter.

With practice your skill will improve. Do your best and pretty soon you will find yourself imagining in more and more senses. Start with what you can do now and you'll do just fine.

One trick that can be very helpful if you have any difficulty with sensory imagining was mentioned as one of the basic how-to principles in our first chapter: Feel free to use your hands when you are "feeling" something in your imagination. Make the motions you would be making if you were actually doing what you imagine yourself doing. I learned this trick from T. X. Barber and it has helped me a lot; if I am picturing myself holding an orange in my hand to peel it, I hold one hand in a cupping gesture as if holding the orange, and I make peeling motions with the other.

Let's work on your imaginary skills some more now. You've covered a lot of serious material, so it's time for fun.

Exercise Three: Exploring Imaginary Experiences
Purpose

To gain more familiarity with guided fantasy.

Method

Guided fantasy—another way of saying imagining along with suggestions, in this case tape-recorded from a script exactly as before.

Script

"I close my eyes and take a few deep breaths, stretch for a moment or two, and let myself relax as I get ready to explore some of the imaginary experiences I can create for myself." (30-second pause.)

"It's August . . . I've been walking in the cruelly hot sun for hours and hours. I'm exhausted and so, so thirsty . . . my lips feel parched . . . so dry and dusty . . . my mouth feels so dry my tongue sticks to the roof of

my mouth . . . so hot and thirsty . . . so thirsty . . . I feel
as if I've been hiking in the hot August sun for hours
and hours. . . .

"Like magic, I find myself at the base of a cliff
. . . out of the naked rock gushes a clear little spring . . .
cool, clear water from the depths of the earth . . . I take
a tin cup and I bend down to scoop up a drink of this
fresh, cold water . . . so icy cold I can see condensation
form on the sides of my cup . . . beads of moisture
trickling down its sides as I raise this tin cup to my lips
. . . I feel it come closer and closer, as if in slow motion
. . . and then I let this cool, refreshing water run over
my lips and into my mouth . . . so wet and cold and
pure and refreshing . . . on my tongue now . . . so wet
and thirst-quenching and satisfyingly cool . . . trickling
down the back of my throat . . . and I swallow . . . feel
this lovely, cool, pure water going down my throat into
my stomach . . . so cool and pure and satisfying . . . it
soothes and relaxes my stomach . . . water makes me
feel so good . . . so full . . . so satisfied . . . so good . . . I
take another drink of this delightfully cool, wet water
. . . I feel it in my mouth . . . water always makes me
feel so good . . . it soothes and relaxes and refreshes me
. . . it feels so good in my mouth and going down my
throat . . . so I take one last sip and then put down my
cup. . . .

"And find myself standing in front of my own
refrigerator at home . . . I am reaching in and taking out
one perfect orange . . . the most beautiful orange ever
imagined . . . I feel this large, juicy, ripe orange nestled
in my hand . . . I marvel at the texture of my orange . . .
at the bumpy orange, waxy feeling of its outer rind . . .
how round and juicy and ripe it feels . . . bursting with
freshness . . . I take my fingers and now begin to peel
this orange . . . reaching in with my fingernail . . .
noticing the little squirts of orange-skin oil . . . smelling

it now, a slightly bitter orange odor . . . as I reach in and peel my orange . . . I can feel the waxy outer rind and now I can also feel the smooth, silky, white, moist inner rind of the orange . . . so smooth and silky. . . . Now I plunge one or two of my fingers deep into the center of the orange where it's cold and moist and cool, and I pull out one or two sections of the orange . . . bright, bright orange crescents bursting with juicy sweet ripeness . . . it smells so good . . . so mouth-wateringly good . . . I can't keep from popping these orange segments into my mouth and biting down on them and letting myself feel their juicy goodness squirting out into my mouth, all over my tongue . . . I feel the sweet juices so cool and sharp on my tongue . . . and I feel the pulp . . . the glorious flavor of a perfect ripe orange in my mouth . . . so juicy and ripe and sweetly delicious . . . I swallow and take another deep bite . . . the juices run down my chin . . . I don't care . . . this is *so* good . . . the fresh fruit taste . . . just sweet enough for me . . . just right . . . a marvelous, delightful treat. . . ."

(From here on, read very slowly, pausing as appropriate.) "It's later now and I feel as if I am walking down a moonlit secret path . . . I am perfectly comfortable, perfectly safe and at ease . . . the temperature is just right . . . I am wearing a loose robe over my naked body . . . feeling perfectly at ease as I walk down this moonlit path . . . the path seems to be made of pure, fine white sand . . . it looks so lovely in the moon's light . . . so clean . . . and it's so soft . . . I must be barefoot. . . .

"I can smell some night-blooming jasmine now . . . I am passing some large bushes . . . silvery green in the moon's light . . . I feel a warm, gentle breeze caressing my face with the perfume of night-blooming jasmine . . . and other tropical flowers . . . the slight odor of salt water . . . I am on a tropical island paradise at night . . . having a stroll down a pure white path . . . feeling every step I take . . . moving my legs . . . swinging my arms . . . peaceful, relaxed, comfortable . . . enjoying myself immensely. . . .

"And I think I hear a bird . . . is it a mockingbird? I don't know . . . some kind of tropical bird . . . it has the sweetest, most lovely song I've ever heard . . . I pause for a moment and close my eyes and just listen to the night bird's song . . . it is the purest, loveliest, sweetest, most thrilling music imaginable . . . it goes deep into my heart and soul . . . filling me with a wondering joy . . . I let the bird sing to me . . . she sings of life and joy and growth and happiness . . . sings the fulfillment of my every dream . . . I stand quietly, reverently, in awe . . . just listening to the night bird's magic song . . . (Pause 15 seconds.) The bird is silent now, she has sung herself out, and I continue strolling down my secret path . . . I pass some pine trees . . . they loom so tall above me . . . I smell their piney fragrance . . . so clean . . . I walk through the tall dark pines . . . like a silent cathedral . . . the path is covered with soft pine needles . . . a soft cushion for my feet . . . [5-second pause] . . . and I'm leaving the pine forest now . . . the moon is settling lower in the western sky . . . before me I see a stream . . . a lazy tropical stream . . . clear and fresh . . . and there's a pool in this stream . . . somebody has carved a stairway down to this bathing pool . . . I walk down the steps of warm, dry stone to the side of the pool. . . .

"I stand at the pool's edge . . . there's nobody around . . . I am comfortable and safe, so I can slip off my robe and stand naked in the tropical moon's light at the side of this natural swimming pool . . . and I slide into the water . . . feeling the warm water caressing my body with its sensuous liquid fingers . . . for a moment I stand at the edge of this pool carved in the living rock, feeling the coolish air above my waist, and the body-temperature water below ... I now plunge into the water—it's never too deep for me to stand—and sink down under the water holding my breath for a moment or two ... it's perfectly safe ... I can do anything in my imagination with dreamlike, effortless ease ... in my imagination, I hold my breath and feel the pressure of the water upon my face ... and then I stand up once again, sucking in a big lungful of the moist, fragrant island air ... and I lie back in the water and allow the water to support my body ... the water rocks me gently for a while as I listen to the lullaby of the trickling stream ... floating on my back and looking up at the stars ... so brilliant ... so far away ... I look up into the velvety tropical night sky as I float in the water and pretend to count the stars [20-second pause]. ...

"I swim back to the pool's edge, where I find a pile of fluffy, soft white towels waiting for me there ... as I dry myself I tell myself I have never felt such a soft towel against my skin ... so soft and absorbent ... such a pleasure to dry myself off with this soft, fluffy towel ... I put my robe on once again and lie down on the mossy bank to one side of this tropical island stream ... looking up at the sky ... the moon sets ... time passes as I lie there ... the sun is beginning to rise. ...

"I notice the first faint lightness in the eastern sky ... then I see the colors ... reds and pinks and oranges and every shade of gold ... huge and orange, the sun climbs above the Pacific Ocean ... the most glorious sunrise I have ever imagined ... all the colors of life ... red and gold and pink and violet and light blue ... more and more brilliant as the sun slowly floats up over the tropical lagoon ... a huge orange orb ... half up ... rising slowly ... I can feel the warmth of its rays on my face now ... the sky brightens ... and I feel myself waking up inside ... I feel so alive ... just wonderful . . . I just feel how good it is to be alive . . . and I open my eyes for real now [open your eyes here] and I return to the everyday world, feeling as if I've been on a two-weeks' vacation in the islands. . . ."

End of script. Retain this tape if you'd like. After listening, write down some notes regarding what you experienced, what images seemed most comfortable and natural to you, which senses came hardest and which came most easily, anything you learned that might help you later, when developing your own scripts.

Now that you've had lots more experience working with your mind in a hypnotic way, why don't you listen again to your session tape from Experiment Six? Do so any time before Experiment Eleven, halfway through the next chapter. After that you'll not need your tape again, so erase it if you'd wish. You can, of course, keep that session and listen to it as many times as you'd like.

FOUR

Doing Strategic Hypnosis

In the last chapters we've concentrated on teaching you the skills of being an effective subject. You've experienced progressive relaxation, a self-administered hypnosis session, and a great variety of suggestions outside hypnosis. So far, however, you've remained a spectator, a recipient of suggestions. In this chapter you'll move on to the other side of hypnosis: how to give yourself suggestions and organize your strategies of self-hypnosis. We'll begin by considering what you are trying to accomplish.

I've discussed this in principle already: You are trying to reconstruct your personal reality, change your definitions of the situation. Every one of us has an internal sense of reality, our definition of *the* situation, a map or model of what the real world is and how it works. The problems you can most easily deal with in hypnosis are problems with your realities: The overeater *knows* he or she cannot really keep away from the excess food making him or her fat; the underachieving student *knows* he or she always messes up on tests.

We've also looked at how your definitions of the situation have a way of becoming self-fulfilling prophecies. Since you routinely, even subconsciously, organize your behavior according to what you consider to be true, your ideas have a very practical impact upon your life.

However, nobody can live without habits, without taking some things for granted. We reduce the things we must do over and over again to habitual routines, otherwise we'd be paralyzed.

Experiment Nine: Doing Things the Hard Way
Purpose

To explore the usefulness of habitual routines.

Method

Read and do, no need to tape.

Directions

There are two parts to this experiment. Do Part 1 and then do Part 2.

Part 1. You are breathing. You've been breathing automatically most of the time, but once you place attention on your breathing, the situation changes. Take your breathing off automatic for a few moments and breathe *consciously*. Make your breathing as regular and as comfortable as it was before you read this paragraph. Once you've tried to do this for a little while, take your attention off breathing and concentrate on writing in your journal some comments on what it was like trying to breathe consciously. (By putting your attention elsewhere, you'll automatically snap back into routine breathing.)

Part 2. Consider the problem of standing up. Let's pretend your mind is a blank and you know absolutely nothing about how to do it. Think of all the little things you must have your body do in order to make it stand up. Think of all the nerve signals you must send flashing up and down between your brain and your muscles, all the feats of coordination and all the millions of movements your muscles have to make— it's mind-boggling. Now, just stand up. Notice how easy it was? Sit down again. This time, try to stand up the hard way, by doing it all consciously, paying attention to each little detail, doing each little act separately. Relax (and sit down if you managed to get up). Jot down some notes about the differences between employing a habitual routine and voluntary, conscious, or self-conscious action.

Breathing and standing up are simple things. What would it be like if each morning you awakened blank? What if you had to figure out all the rules for doing things and then, to get anything done, you had to consciously select and direct each little step required. It took you a long while to learn your routines, but without them you'd be stuck.

You've learned your part in the world of everyday life in about the same way. You've learned how to act like a civilized person, how to do all the little things such a person is expected to do. These things, too, become habitual routines. Like a stage actor, once you master the mechanics of acting and familiarize yourself with the character you are to portray, you can take your attention off these things and devote your full effort to giving a successful performance. Forming habitual routines and constructing realities you can take for granted both serve the purpose of freeing you to concentrate on strategy—on getting things done, rather than all the little detailed actions required to get from here to there.

At first you must conscientiously and self-consciously act out the script or routine. When I first was learning to drive a car, I found it very difficult to keep everything straight in my mind. I had to watch what was going on in front of me through the windshield, be aware of everything happening on either side, and also keep checking the rearview mirror. At the same time, I had to be steering, watching the speedometer, operating the clutch, brake, and gearshift. That's an awful lot to be doing all at once.

Everything required my conscious effort for a while. With practice, it seemed less and less impossible to coordinate all these tasks. Then, as I diligently kept on practicing my driving, more and more of these actions slipped into habitual routines. Now, after years of driving, I can keep my attention on where I am going or even think about something else entirely, and simultaneously continue to do the little things necessary to get there safely. In fact, there are times when I "space out" either in a conversation or internal woolgathering, only to discover that several minutes have passed and I've driven many miles on automatic pilot.

Principles of Strategic Hypnosis

The strategic approach centers around the concept of reality reconstruction. You develop and apply a range of mental tactics by which you can change your definitions of the situation. For all practical purposes, *you are your acts.* That is the real definition of the situation—not what you think you believe, not what you feel you should believe, not what you believe you feel, or what you think you believe. It's what you actually do that counts.

The first principle of strategic hypnosis, then, is that *the way to be changed is to act changed.* Often, however, in order to change your act you need to change your ideas about reality and what is "only natural" for you. You must not only change what you do in the external, social world, but also what you do inside yourself—those habitual mental acts by which you have created and now maintain your realities. Therefore, you must act to change both what you are telling yourself in your background thinking and also how you feel about things.

The second principle is that *when your imaginations (what you believe or define to be so) come into conflict with your will (what you consciously choose to feel or do), your imaginations always win.* So long as you are fighting yourself, you can't win. In order to obtain what you want for yourself, you need to change how you imagine things to be. That is, you must adjust your inner realities to your present needs.

Even our problems tend to spring from our innate practicality. Therefore, third, *in order to understand our problems, we must look at their practical dimension.*

I can best explain with an example. The other day I received a telephone inquiry from a man who thought hypnosis could help him. He told me he wanted to get his act together. He was most concerned about smoking cigarettes. His girl friend had recently died from severe health problems compounded by her heavy drinking, and he was starting to worry about what he was doing to himself. He was also working full-time managing a coffee house, taking courses at the university, writing one play and two novels.

"Ah," I remarked. "You're under a lot of pressure and the stress is getting to you."

Without missing a beat, he replied, "Right on—but at least I don't have an ulcer."

This guy is sharp. Not only is he doing more than two ordinary people but he's dealing with more craziness than I can relate here. Somehow he gets by. How? By chain-smoking tobacco.

His habit does something for him: It helps him get by. To just get him to quit smoking would be no real help at all. It would be like taking away the crutches from someone whose leg is still broken. This is what I mean by taking into account the practical dimension.

Changing your life is more than a matter of positive thinking. It requires practical good sense.

Unless you can translate your goals into routine action, you've accomplished nothing worthwhile. The real work of self-improvement is learning to act transformed when you are out there, on the spot, actually living your life.

How do you that? *Using verbal suggestion, you*

develop imaginings in order to get at and shape your feelings. This is our fourth principle. You begin, usually, by relaxing yourself so you can let go and imagine without blocking yourself. Then you tell yourself what you want to become your new mental habit. To make it real for yourself, you then use your imagining to construct a fantasy of yourself being, feeling, and acting that way as if it were already your normal, unremarkable routine. By practicing your new reality in your imagination, you make it your habit.

Shaping habitual feelings in this way takes advantage of the fact that you tend to act in line with your gut-level definitions of the situation automatically, without thinking about it. This strategy permits you, in effect, to program your own spontaneous conduct. Once you've aligned your thinking and feeling with what you want for yourself—your will—it becomes "only natural" to act transformed.

The alternative to establishing new ideas for your habitual routines in this way was stated by William James: "Never suffice an exception to occur till the new habit is securely rooted in your life." That, however, is a hard way to go about it. If it were no problem to just act differently, most cf us in the counseling and therapy professions would be out of a job!

The problem is that just barging ahead and trying to act differently creates all manner of double binds and consequent strain for yourself. The harder you try, the more you tend to trip yourself up.

This is our fifth principle, described by Kroger as the "law of reversed effort." *The harder you try to force it, the less likely will be your success.* The way around this problem, as Kroger puts it, is to use your imagination power rather than your willpower. In order to change your act most easily and effectively, change what you mean by your actions and what the objects of your actions mean to you.

Nonetheless, it still makes practical good sense to follow James's advice, as best you can, to:

> . . . accumulate all the possible circumstances which shall re-enforce the right motives; put yourself assiduously in conditions that encourage the new way; make engagements incompatible with the old; take a public pledge, if the case allows; in short, envelop your resolution with every aid you know.

To change your performances, change your habits of self-interaction. But how do you actually go about creating a new mental habit? How else than by *practice!*

That's how you make or break any habit of any kind. By practicing thinking, feeling, and imagining in the new, desired way—with the help of your self-hypnosis techniques—you establish the new definition of the situation as a reality for yourself. Then, as James suggests, by practicing your new reality in daily life it becomes what you and everybody else can simply take for granted as "how you really are."

First, as I've indicated, it is most expedient to reconstruct your inner realities on the principle that *any idea or goal upon which you focus or practice in imaginative rehearsal often enough over long enough a time tends to become your spontaneous tendency.* To complete the process, you then need only to allow yourself to release that inclination in your actual conduct. In fact, you will probably find yourself doing so spontaneously.

The Forms of Suggestion

To apply these six principles of strategic hypnosis in your own self-hypnosis, you will use some combination of three basic forms or tactics of suggestion. Corresponding to the three mental processes I've described, these are direct suggestion, guided fantasy, and symbolism.

Direct suggestion involves just what you'd expect

from the name: verbal statements used in hypnosis to define situations or prompt specified actions. "You are getting sleepy" is a classic example. In the old days, suggestions of this type were the primary tactic of hypnotists. I suspect a majority of those practicing today still rely most heavily on this method.

Used in the old-fashioned manner, the suggestion is actually a command. So long as one can get the subject to believe that response to suggestions is involuntary, this tactic may be quite efficacious. Many professional hypnotists do try to create such a definition of the situation. If they can bring it off, telling the subject what to do and believe may work out well.

Whatever the case, that tactic is totally alien to the strategic approach. Outright commands, by and large, are perhaps the least effective hypnotic technique. They literally invite resistance—and there are far more powerful ways of using words.

In strategic self-hypnosis we use direct suggestion solely for *prompting* ourselves or *to define a situation* in terms of meanings and expectations for what we are experiencing, have experienced, or will experience in the future.

The prompting function is often obvious, since we are accustomed to use words to communicate what we'd like another to think or do. Every suggestion either asks you to think, feel, do, or imagine something, or identifies how to understand or interpret what is going on or is about to happen. You might like to go over the script for Experiment Four, identifying for yourself the different ways in which statements were used in that exercise.

Guided fantasy or visualization has become the mainstay of the "new hypnosis." With visualizations, you can lead the subject to create real-as-life imaginary experiences that involve and channel his or her total self-interactions. Most important of all, you can use this process to get at feelings, the gut-level definition of the situation.

You can get the subject to respond in his or her self-interactions just as he or she would to real-life situations. As you may have been learning for yourself in the experiments and exercises of our last chapter, this response can go deeper than what I am describing as the mental process of feeling. You can actually get at and strategically exploit the full range of psychosomatic or mind-body linkages in order to develop anesthesia, control blood flow, etc.

By directing your words to create and guide fantasy, you can almost play yourself like a musical instrument. As Kroger points out, by this method you can bring back and recombine, however you'd like, any sensations you have ever experienced.

In practice, you will use verbal statements to guide your construction of fantasy experiences. The imaginations you create in this fashion can be used in any number of ways. Your primary means of controlling your visualizations and making them work for you will be using further verbal suggestion to define the meaning of that experience.

You might want to turn back to Exercise Three and study the various ways in which guided fantasy was employed and how direct suggestions were used to construct and guide those visualizations. It would be particularly valuable to go over your notes from that exercise to see what sort of visualizations worked best for you and which worked least well.

Our third tactic, *symbolism,* is really more of a facilitator than an actual method. You use metaphors, images, or other devices to make an imaginary connection between things, ideas, or events. This has been raised to the level of an art in the "indirect suggestion" techniques of the late Milton Erickson.

As you'll be using symbolism, however, it will mainly be in conjunction with the other two methods. Specific tactics will be discussed when appropriate.

Two symbolic devices are worth brief mention here.

You can use the verbal formula "more and more" to make anything seem to be becoming more like you want it to be. For example: "Each and every new day I find myself coping with what comes up in a more and more calm, relaxed, effective way." Alternatively, you can use the "as if" statement: "I feel as if I am a butterfly flitting and fluttering about without a care in the world." Both tactics help you ignore objective reality and also override your internal sense of how things are and must remain—they help you get into the imaginary.

The Secret of Effective Visualization

There is a simple trick that will allow you to get the most out of working with guided fantasy:

Experiment Ten: Putting Yourself in the Scene
Purpose

To observe how you locate yourself within the actual situation.

Method

Read and do, no need to tape.

Directions

Take a few deep breaths and close your eyes. Let yourself just relax for a moment. Now open your eyes and observe your surroundings. How do you orient yourself to your physical setting? What cues do you use to get the sense of where you are? What are you noticing that gives you the sense of being in this particular time and place as opposed to somewhere else? Do you see yourself? What parts of your body and your attire can you actually notice? What parts of your environment are you actually aware of? What lies in your field of vision? What do you hear, feel, smell, or see?

Once you've considered these questions for a while, jot down some notes about how you locate yourself where you are, what you actually perceive about the situation in which you find yourself, and what you

> have discovered about what it takes to get the sense of really being there.

Were you surprised to discover how you are only aware of *selected* bits and pieces of the world around you? These are mainly sensory aspects of your surroundings— things you can directly see, feel, hear, or otherwise perceive. Even then, you barely notice most of the world around you—although you *know* it's there.

One of the most important things you don't see is yourself. You are not actually in the picture. As I am typing these words, I orient myself primarily by my visual perception, secondarily through sounds and the feelings of my fingers and hands moving. I am also, though barely, aware of the feeling of my clothing against my skin and of the pressure of my bottom against the seat of my chair.

When I look out of my eyes, I see a limited field of vision. I see my fingers, hands, and part of my forearms in my peripheral vision, particularly as they move. I see the wall in front of me about as far up as my hairline and a yard or two to either side. The quality of the light tells me the lights are on in this room. The air is slightly cool. I can hear the wind outside my window. I take in these limited cues and reconstruct mentally a sense of the actual context within which I find myself. That's how I more or less automatically locate myself in this scene.

The trick is to do the same thing in your imagination. You'll rarely get very far by telling yourself something like "I am now lying on a beach in Hawaii." The scene will remain intellectual, unreal. But if you sketch for yourself all the little sensory cues appropriate to your imaginary surroundings, you'll seem to actually be there. The rule is *prompt yourself by focusing on anything you could actually be perceiving if you were really in that scene.*

Unless you are looking at your reflection in a mirror or your image in a photo, movie, or television sceen, you would never see your body face-on. However, sometimes you might want to imagine yourself from that external viewpoint. To do so, very gently "sketch" in your mind the back of your head or a vague outline of a face like your own, and suggest to yourself that "the picture will become clearer and clearer as I notice the—" and then go on to your contextual cues.

A form of this tactic is commonly employed in forensic hypnosis—working with victims and witnesses of crime—or with children. The hypnotist has the subject visualize a television show and then describes the scene, leaving the subject him or herself very vague: ". . . and, standing by this pine tree, you might notice someone who looks very much like yourself watching the cars in the parking lot. . . . She notices a car speeding off. . . . What color might that car be?"

Normally, you need only describe to yourself the main sensory details you would perceive if you were there in the scene. Don't try to put yourself in the picture. Rather, *build up the feelings and sensations of being in the scene and it will become realistic for you—you will seem to be actually there.* What you are doing is, in effect, to first create the feelings of being there and then allowing the idea that "this is really happening" to follow in due course. Let's see how it works for you, okay?

Experiment Eleven: Building Up a Visualization
Purpose
　　To practice applying the secret of effective visualization.
Method
　　Guided fantasy—tape and follow exactly as before.
Directions
　　In this experiment, you are going to make up your own script. Start by thinking for a minute—what would be a particularly safe and relaxing scene for you? Many people like to imagine themselves basking on a tropical beach, loafing by a mountain stream, or curling up by a crackling fire. There is no reason to limit the

details in your scene to how it would be in the real world but rather, make it an ideal scene of relaxation—one that is absolutely perfect.

Once you've thought up the scene you'd like to work with, write out your script, word for word. It should take about three minutes to read—possibly three pages written out longhand.

Tips:

1. All you have to do is describe the scene exactly as you'd like it to be for yourself. Put into it all the things you could actually see, hear, feel, smell, or otherwise notice if you were really in that situation, even if it's a totally imaginary one. Put in all the sensory cues you can think up, not just the names of things. For example, not "I watch the fire," but "I stare into a merry fire crackling in the fireplace, watching the bright orange and red flames licking upward, sending out showers of little glowing sparks. . . ."

2. Prompt yourself by connecting what you're imagining with ideas for relaxing: "I feel the sun's warm rays shining on my face, so soothing, so relaxing . . . I can feel all the little tensions being washed away more and more as I hear each new wave breaking on the shore . . . washing through my mind . . . rinsing away all thought, all tightness and tension. . . ."

3. As implied, use physical or behavioral terms whenever possible. Note that, in this last example, I speak of "tightness and tension" rather than just "stress," "washing through my mind" rather than "in my mind." This is the sort of language I am referring to.

4. Useful phrases: "I can feel" or "I can feel my body," "more and more," "it feels so good." Useless phrases: "it is," "I will," and "I try."

Don't worry about writing a perfect script. Don't spend more than a half hour working on it—ten minutes is more like it. Just fix in your mind the sort of thing you want to have in your scene and write down whatever comes to mind, adding suggestions as appropriate. If it feels right, it is right, okay? Then record your script as you've been doing in other experiments, sit back, and imagine along with your voice.

Afterward, write down some comments on how it went, what seemed to work best, how you might change or improve your scripts in the future, anything you feel you've learned from this experiment about working with suggestions.

Congratulations. You now know all you need to know about working with suggestions, at least in principle. It's time to put it all together. In the following exercise, therefore, you will have an opportunity to experience a session of strategic hypnosis transcribed from sessions I have used with clients seeking to explore their human potentialities. You will even record it in the second person to get the flavor of my session style.

At this point, you will want to keep your progressive-relaxation tape and record this session on the reverse of its cassette. Any other recordings can be kept if you'd like, but feel free to record over them (the cassette player will automatically erase material already on the tape). To ensure that you don't erase the tapes you want to keep for permanent use, knock out the little tabs as instructed on the cassette box (or ask someone to show you how to do this).

Exercise Four: Strategic Hypnosis for Human-Potentialities Training

Purpose

To practice working with strategic hypnosis and to begin learning some practical techniques.

Method

Hypnosis—thinking, feeling, and imagining along with your tape.

Script

"Let's begin. Please make your body comfortable, so you can really relax. With your eyes still open, find a spot on the ceiling just above your hairline and stare at it with all your might. Let's find out what your eyes are going to do. They might want to blink and water or cross or close . . . just let your eyes do whatever they want to do while you stare at your point and listen to my suggestions. Keep on staring and seeing how you are going to surprise yourself as you enter hypnosis in your own personal way. All we know for sure is that you'll soon be feeling a wonderful, soothing, relaxing sensation beginning somewhere in your body and spreading throughout your body and your mind if you let it . . . why don't you?

"Keep staring with your eyes and just remember for a moment what you would most like to get out of this session . . . think of your goals for self-hypnosis . . . perhaps begin saying to yourself in your mind, 'I *can* do it, I'm free!' over and over and over . . . as you begin now to relax, you can feel yourself feeling more and more comfortable . . . letting go . . . more and more calm and receptive now . . . feeling more and more curious about what's going to happen next . . . why don't you let your eyes close now if they're still open and roll your eyeballs up as if you were staring at the center of your forehead . . . good . . . now take a deep breath and hold it in your lungs until you have to let go and then just breathe all the way out and, as slowly as you can, let your eyeballs roll back down to their relaxed, natural resting position . . . slowly . . . feeling yourself letting go now, more and more . . . it feels so heavenly to relax . . . so good . . . to just think, feel, and imagine along with my words . . . so good . . . it makes you feel so good . . . and you begin to notice that something very wonderful, very interesting and desirable is occurring somewhere in your body and mind now, or perhaps it is about to happen in another moment or two as you feel yourself entering what we call a hypnotic frame of mind. . . . (10-second pause.)

"You want to really get into it so you can get the most possible benefit out of your hypnosis, so I am going to ask you to squeeze and then relax your eyes over and over while, at the same time, you count down from——[here insert the number representing your age plus two—if you're thirty-three years old, you'd use thirty-five, etc.] . . . what you will do is say the number as you squeeze your eyes as tightly shut as you can, and as you say and hear the number also picture it like the number on a birthday cake or a number written in chalk on a blackboard . . . once you imagine seeing the number, then relax your eyes and as you relax your eyes let the number go away . . . vanish . . . erase or forget the number from your mind as you feel yourself drifting deeper and deeper into a dreamy hypnotic state . . . then squeeze your eyes again, say and picture the next number down, relax your eyes, and go deeper still . . . it's real easy . . . keep on doing this until you get all the way down to zero or until your eyes or mind won't do it any longer because you're becoming too dreamy, deep, relaxed . . . don't worry about a thing . . . you'll always go deep enough to get what you need out of this session . . . when you've reached zero or can't continue counting down and squeezing your eyes, just drift and dream along with my suggestions . . . you're going deeper and deeper and deeper with every breath you breathe in for the rest of this session . . . and with every breath you blow out you're breathing away more and more tightness, tension, self-consciousness . . . cleansing yourself of everything and anything that could hold you back from achieving your goals from strategic self-hypnosis . . . are you ready? You want to go as deep as you possibly can in this or any other session, so you can just let yourself, okay?

"Here we go, all the way down into your hypnosis . . . squeeze your eyes tightly closed right now, picture and say the number [your age plus 2] . . . relax your eyes and forget that number . . . erase it . . . blank it out from your mind . . . good . . . now squeeze your eyes again . . . tightly . . . picture and say the next number down [your age plus 1], relax your eyes and forget that number . . . erase it and go deeper . . . good . . . it feels so good to drift into a hypnotic frame of mind now . . . squeeze your eyes again . . . this time, picture and say [your age] . . . relax your eyes, erase or forget that number . . . feeling the hypnosis now . . . more and more . . . and once more squeeze your eyes tightly shut . . . picture and say the number [age minus 1], relax your eyes, forget the number, and let yourself keep on drifting deeper and deeper into your hypnosis as you keep on squeezing and relaxing your eyes, picturing and erasing the next number down . . . until you're deep enough and find yourself just breathing in and breathing out, more and more dreamily drifting along with my voice . . . you will always be able to hear and respond to my suggestions or anything occurring around you that really needs your attention . . . you can always bring yourself back to full waking consciousness by counting up to ten . . . so it's safe . . . it's perfectly okay for you to let go completely and just drift deeper and deeper . . . feeling the lovely sensations of your hypnosis growing stronger and stronger for you . . . easier and easier for you to imagine and do . . . noises, stray thoughts, distractions just pass through your mind like little vacuum cleaners, leaving you more involved, more clear and peaceful, calm and relaxed . . . it feels so good to just let go and to drift into your deepest hypnosis . . . now I will be silent and it may seem like minutes or it may seen like hours or seconds or years and years of wonderful, peaceful time . . . a time of healing and building your strength . . . a time of letting go of the past and letting yourself just be . . . you don't have to think about a thing now . . . it's all okay . . . you can feel more and more confident that you'll get what you hoped for from strategic self-hypnosis . . . that you can really do it now . . . just feel yourself breathing in and breathing out as you drift deeper and deeper with every beat of your heart . . . it feels so good . . . sooooooo gooooood. . . ." (3-minute silence.)

(Whispering at first and quickly growing louder, back to your normal calm voice) "Further and further into the calmness, peace, and relaxation now . . . let yourself feel like a caterpillar floating in a womb cocoon of deep relaxation and perfect peace . . . soon I will ask you to awaken from your session and when I do you will be ready to grow out of more and more of the ways of thinking and feeling and behaving that held you back . . . you feel more and more ready now . . . you feel it starting to begin . . . I will ask you to awaken and you'll be ready . . . and this and every time you end a session of hypnosis or self-hypnosis, you will have gone deeper with more and more benefit and ease and you'll find that you've already moved further and further along toward your goals for yourself . . . and you'll feel each time you end a session of hypnosis or self-hypnosis . . . and each new morning as you awaken you'll feel yourself reborn, renewed, refreshed . . . seeing more and more clearly with the fresh, unspoiled eyes of a child . . . seeing things in proper perspective more and more . . . now discovering more and more the joy and wonder in living . . . the little miracles of being alive . . . but for now, why don't you just forget about yourself and your real life and let yourself float along with my voice . . . dreamily . . . feeling more and more certain that you are okay now . . . that you can do it . . . nothing can ever again stop you or block you or distract you from becoming in all ways that person you choose to be . . . because you are becoming more and more fully alive . . . less and less like a robot . . . more and more that complete, strong, calm, effective, cheerful, healthy, positive, fulfilled, compulsion-free, and happy person you have always hoped it was in you to be . . . and it is . . . you can feel it now . . . feel the joy and the freedom and the power growing within you . . . ready to burst through . . . you can feel yourself moving into the future now . . . letting go of the past and moving into the future you are now creating for yourself by your positive, constructive, spontaneous thoughts and actions . . . living in the present time and allowing yourself to be and feel and think and act the ways you choose for yourself because you want to . . . you are free . . . it feels so good to feel free . . . you feel yourself on the verge of breaking through now . . . into new power and joy and freedom and aliveness . . . leaving behind all your no-longer-needed caterpillar tastes and needs and habits and appetites and limitations and frustrations . . . it's safe to let go and feel yourself now about to awaken as a beautiful, strong, graceful, slender, joyous butterfly soaring powerfully, lightly, up, up, up toward the sunlight of your dreams and goals and hopes and desires . . . feel yourself anticipating your new freedom . . . feel the new power surging through your veins . . . the first hints of your new certainty and joy in living . . . but for now, why don't you just let yourself be like a caterpillar floating in a womb cocoon of perfect relaxation, perfect peace and stillness . . . absolute safety and freedom. . . . (10-second pause.)

"As you drift and relax you begin to daydream along with my voice . . . fantasizing about how it will be for you as you actually accomplish one, two, three of your most important remaining goals or objectives in your life . . . you can almost see a three-dimensional movie of yourself as if you were already seeing and feeling these things coming true . . . it is a very detailed all-senses movie of how it could be . . . it shows you for certain that you are doing it . . . you can see and feel yourself making your goals come true as you watch . . . you notice all the little details in the scene . . . sounds and sights and smells and feelings telling you this is real . . . and there may be other people in the movie with you . . . see what they're wearing and saying and doing . . . now see and feel this vision all around you . . . yourself in the dream . . . a prophetic dream as real as life itself . . . feel how good it feels to have your goals and dreams and hopes for yourself come true . . . really enjoying your success . . . feeling so proud of yourself . . . why not let yourself keep on experiencing this dream, this vision of your success the way you would want it to be . . . like the best of all possible dreams. . . .

"As you drift along you feel you are actually learning to be this new calm, relaxed, able, and efficient you . . . more and more calm, confident, positive, alert, fully alive in your everyday life . . . able to sleep restfully and peacefully at night . . . calm, confident, positive, and able to cope at all times, in any or all circumstances . . . whatever happens . . . see yourself dealing with problems calmly and matter-of-factly now . . . step by step, piece by piece, doing what you feel you should and could in those circumstances, as best you can . . . and then you let go of the matter in your body and in your mind and you relax and flow on to the next thing in your life . . . still calm and relaxed . . . less and less like a robot . . . more and more fully alive . . . waking up in your life . . . taking charge of yourself . . . you don't have to strain or force it, it comes naturally now, more and more naturally each and every new day . . . you find yourself being at all times, in all circumstances, that person you want to be . . . yourself. . . .

"And when something comes up you must deal

with, you pause for a split second . . . before you act . . . you might want to take a deep breath and say 'zero' to yourself to clear your mind and calm yourself . . . and then breathe out, knowing you're okay, that you can do it . . . before you act or react, you pause for a moment . . . you breathe in and say 'zero' to yourself and as you breathe out you can see the situation clearly, in perspective . . . and you can trust yourself now . . . you pause and say 'zero' and you observe clearly how it actually is, not how you might have thought or worried or expected it might be . . . but as it actually happens to be, and you can see the best way to do something about it . . . to make the situation work out okay, as you want it to work out . . . you do what you feel you can or should do at the time and you do your very best and you can accept what you've done as your very best under those circumstances and let go and relax once again and flow on to the next things, the next opportunities to act in your life . . . starting to really live . . . more and more spontaneously that self you choose to be . . . you don't have to try any longer . . . because you are allowing yourself to be naturally free. . . .

"Each and every new day brings new surprises as you discover yourself becoming and being in fact more and more these ways you yourself choose to be . . . think about what you want out of life [10-second pause] . . . to make this come true for you, you are determined from this moment forth to take care of yourself and to care for yourself . . . properly, in all ways . . . to take the best, most appropriate care of your body and your health . . . to feed your body properly, to give yourself the exercise you need . . . it feels so good to take care of yourself properly . . . it's so rewarding to care for yourself . . . it feels so good. . . .

"Squeeze your eyes tightly shut now, relax your eyes, and go deeper . . . feel yourself becoming more and more truly alive . . . full of life and joy and health and strength and abilities more than you ever dreamed possible . . . you can feel yourself opening up inside now . . . allowing your self to emerge as a new person . . . the self you have always wanted to be if only . . . if you could let yourself . . . and now you can and you do and it's really happening . . . your mind finds the best way for you to deal with each new situation, demand, person or thought or feeling, right then and there . . . on the spot . . . you pause, say 'zero' to yourself, and allow yourself to deal with it to the very best of your ability, remaining calm, clear, and focused as you do so, and then you take your mind off that thing or project or person or problem or event until the next time you can or should do something about it . . . you can absolutely trust yourself now . . . you can allow yourself to function to your fullest ability . . . because you feel okay about yourself now . . . because you've looked deep inside of yourself and found that you are all right . . . more okay than you could ever have believed . . . you can feel this now . . . go ahead . . . you can feel the truth of these words and you can really begin to live life to its fullest. . . .

"You find that with every session of hypnosis or self-hypnosis more and more wonderful things happen for you . . . one surprising thing is this: whenever—starting right now, this very moment—you do anything you should feel good about, whenever you rise to the demands of the situation and make things go right for yourself, whenever you use your techniques of strategic self-hypnosis in your life, you get the most wonderful, pleasurable, sensual, almost sexual, good feelings of comfort and joy and pride and energy and strength, calmness and satisfaction, ease and peace of mind, a rush of unbelievable pleasure flooding through your body and mind . . . feel it right now . . . you feel this same reassuring, empowering, liberating feeling just like a reflex every single time you stand up for yourself and assert yourself, how and when and as you judge appropriate . . . feel it growing stronger . . . you feel this same liberating and empowering feeling every single time you turn down a chance to give in, back down, or otherwise blow it for yourself . . . it grows stronger and stronger now, unbelievable pleasure . . . you feel it like a reflex every single time you act in a way you feel is right and proper for you . . . it proves you are not a robot. . . .

"You are free . . . allowing yourself to live to your fullest potential now . . . in your mind you begin to see a lovely magical butterfly . . . wings glimmering with every color imaginable . . . you feel that you are well on your way now . . . it is good to be alive . . . to begin to really live . . . starting right now, this very moment . . . you can feel it . . . a change in yourself . . . a change you have been waiting for all your life . . . and you feel like a butterfly emerging from the cocoon at long last . . . spreading your new wings in the warm, wonderful sunlight . . . strong with life and joy . . . calmness, peace, power, and self-fulfillment . . . are you ready? You are about to really wake up, I mean *really* wake up into new freedom, new joy, into a whole new life, the new life you are now building for yourself. . . .

"In a few moments it will be time to open your eyes and end this session. How would you like to feel after this session? Wouldn't you like to feel wide awake, comfortable, peaceful, yet alert . . . deeply refreshed . . . in the highest of spirits? . . . You can feel that good or even better . . . but first, for a moment, think of what you would most like to have gotten out of this session [15-second pause] . . . All these things can be yours now—just take a deep breath, breathe out and, out loud, count up from one to ten. After saying 'ten,' open your eyes, and you may find yourself not only wide awake and comfortable but feeling some really positive changes in yourself and your attitudes toward life . . . and you will know that you are really and truly on the road to success, to the fulfillment of your hopes and goals for yourself. Here goes—right now, if you've not already done so, count yourself up out of this session and into being fully alive."

End of script. At this point, you don't have to analyze this script. Treat it like poetry or an abstract painting. After the first time you have listened to this tape, do not try to recall what happened or analyze it. Rather, let it just sink in; 24 to 48 hours later, play your tape once more. Wait a minute or two after that session, and then you can open your notebook and make some notes about your experiences. Play this tape at least twice more before doing Exercise Six. Retain it and use whenever you want some reinforcement in the future.

FIVE

Organizing Your Plan of Action

You will be using strategic self-hypnosis in at least three ways. You will employ this approach to do things with your body and mind right now, in the present time. You will also learn how to use your self-hypnosis skills to resolve problems hanging you up in your life and to set yourself up for maximum performance and success in the things and situations you must deal with or do in the relatively near future.

Your most important use, however, will be actually shaping your own self, your day-to-day performances, by changing your realities. Your objectives will be to learn to act more freely, according to your own purposes and preferences; to be able to act as you'd prefer, "naturally" and spontaneously, without conscious effort or stress; and to master skills and tactics enabling you to operate at your highest potential, so that you can actively help yourself get what you want in life. I believe these objectives are nicely summed up by the term *self-management.*

In this chapter you will lay the groundwork for attaining better self-management. In effect, you will be organizing your overall plan of action for applying the strategic method to your own needs and objectives.

When we discussed the principles of this approach in the previous chapter, I gave you the idea that the easy and effectual way to accomplish better self-management was to use your imagining to change what is "only natural" for you. I said that you can do this by changing the meanings things and actions hold for you so that your spontaneous thinking and feeling work with you and not against you. This approach is based upon the observation that you subconsciously organize your behavior on the basis of your definitions of the situation, and that your actions in the real, objective world reflect your acting out the script supplied by those understandings.

As we shift into a practical gear, I should slightly modify what I have said previously. There are, you see, some practical limits to what you can or would even want to change. It is true that *you are your act.* However, there are some ways of living and behaving that can never "be you."

Not only are you your acts, but you are also, in a very deep way, *yourself.* You have an individuality, a basic sense of identity that cannot be ignored. Regardless of the theory involved, this is a fact of life.

How, then, can you tell what you can or should change about yourself or your life? How do you decide?

Let me ease your mind on this point. You don't have to worry about it; just stick with what you feel is right, proper, desirable, and appropriate. It's as easy as that. In all things, *trust yourself and your basic sense of what is right for you.* This is the seventh principle of strategic hypnosis. Keep it in mind and you'll never go wrong.

Hypnosis and Willpower

Two concepts are conspicuously absent from that list of principles. One is *doing it by hypnosis.* The other is *willpower.* Let me explain.

First of all, you can't do anything "by hypnosis." Hypnosis is no cure for anything, let alone everything. Hypnosis is a frame of mind, an enormously useful situation that can be very, very helpful in learning new skills, overcoming disabilities, and solving problems. Its role is that of a facilitator, not a therapy.

We use hypnosis to facilitate your success in acquiring better self-management. It is a way of making your task enormously easier for yourself, perhaps making some things possible that you would not otherwise be able to accomplish. However, it is no substitute for your honest effort. In this world, to get anything you must work for it—there's no way to avoid that fact. The best you can do is to make your work easier and more pleasant for you.

Suggestion is not a cure-all either. Like hypnosis, it is but a tool.

Beware of snake oil under whatever guise it is sold. There exists no painless cure-all for problems in living, no one-size-fits-all Philosophers' Stone by which we convert ourselves to instant golden perfection. I wish there were, but there is none.

Do you, then, need willpower to attain your goals? If you don't have enough willpower, can you get it through hypnosis?

Heck, I don't even know what willpower means! I think I know where the idea comes from, however. This miraculous quality seems to represent deeply engrained traces of America's Puritan or Calvinist heritage. In that religious tradition, so crucial in shaping our nation's earliest history, the world was considered the testing ground of the devout. Great stress was placed upon overcoming the flesh and the temptations of the flesh. This became a moral imperative in our secular culture, hence our modern glorification of willpower.

Myths, however, usually have a core of truth. Removing its cultural veneer, I think willpower boils down to good old applied stubbornness. I'm sure you know how to be stubborn at times. You were once a child and, as every parent learns, all children exhibit this attitude in the course of growing up.

While we rely on imagination power and not will-power, we do mobilize and use the quality of stubbornness in our strategic approach. The method we employ is to reawaken the stubborn, playful, spontaneous little child yet lurking within you. We turn these childlike qualities to your own adult advantage.

None is more potent than the attitude of stubborn-ness: "Nyah, nyah, I won't—can't make me!" This lies at the root of your ability to voluntarily block actions, to refuse to do what you feel or are told you are supposed to do. It's not so much naughtiness as basic assertion of your self-deter-minism. There is enormous power in the attitude of "I refuse," a power you can use to translate your own prefer-ences and desires for yourself into behavioral reality. This liberty is an essential condition for self-management, this fact that you don't have to be or do or feel anything you don't want to. But it's not, when you examine it closely, a matter of willpower—it's a matter of your innate liberty to take charge of yourself.

The Stress Factor

Nine times out of ten, what you are bugged by enough to do something about it through self-hypnosis boils down to *stress.* Once neglected, this concept has risen to the fore-front of the revolution in health care, as seen in the emer-gence of the field of behavioral medicine and the closely related holistic health movement.

Technically, stress describes a situation wherein an organism must adjust its internal functioning in order to restore physical balances or act to cope adaptively with external circumstances threatening its survival. In self-help, our major concern is specifically with the fight-or-flight response, in which you gear up for action by raising your heartbeat and respiratory rate, secrete adrenaline, and switch your bodily energies to the task of tensing your skeletal muscles.

While you can sometimes use the nervous energy created in this response creatively in your life, the basic reaction is simply not appropriate to modern life. You can't cope with threats by either fleeing or fighting. Whom do you attack when you are simply inundated by a ceaseless onslaught of threats, pressures, conflicting demands, and still more news about yet other things to worry about? High stress is simply a condition of modern civilized life; it only harms you to keep your panic button jammed in the "on" position under these circumstances.

Is it surprising, then, that the practical dimension of so many of our common modern-day problems is related to stress? Very often, those actions by which you manage or reduce stress lead on a longer-term basis to the problems you are seeking to resolve by learning self-hypnosis. I'm sure you can think of your own examples of how stress affects your life.

One thing puzzled me when I first started clinical practice. Clients reported the identical feelings and problems when they were bored, lonely, or had too little with which to cope as when they were overburdened, under pressure, or threatened. Furthermore, some people seemed to thrive under high levels of stress that would drive you or me crazy.

I eventually realized that each of us has a certain range of tolerance for degrees of stress in our lives. You are comfortable within a certain spectrum of threats, pressures, levels of activity, problems, and tasks to deal with. If your tolerance is *exceeded*, you say you can't take the pressure and feel under stress. However, if you go *below* your comfort range, you say that you can't stand that either. Under such conditions you either create meaningless activity for yourself or prepare for disaster by stress responses, engage in habitual behaviors designed to relieve stress feelings, and tend to feel anxious or depressed.

Plus *or* minus stress, in other words, gets to you. It's just the same as for mechanical devices; too much or too little fuel-to-air mixture in the carburetor of your automobile causes its engine to conk out.

One of your goals in self-management training, therefore, should be to expand your *range of comfort* with regard to underloads and overloads of stress. At the same time, you will use your self-hypnosis to relax yourself on a daily basis, and you will also work to better manage your responses to specific stress-producing relationships or situations that you must deal with in day-to-day life.

It is particularly important to recognize the structural or built-in basis of so much of the stress you must cope with in your everyday life. Corporations, small businesses, public agencies, and entire professions such as nursing, sales, and air traffic control by their very nature load you with extremely high levels of stress. In such a situation there is no reason to feel guilty or personally responsible for the fact that you are feeling or "compulsively" reacting to undue stress.

It's rarely possible to run away from these situations. What you can do, however, is to learn how not to let it get at you so badly, and to learn how to let go of that stress and tension once you leave the work setting. But face it—the situation itself is crazy, not you. If you feel you have been acting inappropriately in response to that stress, consider that whatever you have been doing has at least enabled you to get by. Now you can learn how to do something better about it.

Relaxation as a Strategy

The antidote to stress is to relax. Relaxation is always an aim in self-hypnosis. However, let's clarify what we do and do not mean by relaxation.

The same word is used to denote two rather different sorts of experiences. The first is a condition of not being tense, anxious, ill at ease, or in a flight-or-fight response. It's really a state of *calm.* In this sense, we are talking about your optimal state of balance, in which you can think and act most freely, with maximum coordination between mind and body, without self-imposed resistance or unwonted physical tension, one in which you can most effectively bring to bear your fullest potentialities.

The second meaning of relaxation describes a far more intense physiological state of *complete relaxation.* This is what you experienced with Exercise One, progressive relaxation. Dr. Herbert Benson, an eminent Harvard cardiologist, has studied the therapeutic benefits of complete relaxation for stress-related disorders such as high blood pressure. He has found that complete relaxation triggers a relaxation response directly opposite to the flight-or-fight response of stress.

Strategic hypnosis employs profound relaxation in three ways. We elicit this relaxation response on a regular basis for its many psychosomatic benefits. As a tool, we employ deep relaxation to facilitate the cognitive restructuring necessary to cease thinking and feeling like an adult firmly anchored in "reality," so that you can slip into the hypnotic frame of mind. The rule is, *when you are deeply relaxed, it becomes much, much easier to let go and throw yourself wholeheartedly into an imaginary experience.* For this effect, however, it is mandatory that you relax both mind and body.

Our third use directly relates to self-management. You can't live completely relaxed all the time. However, one of your basic objectives in strategic self-hypnosis is to establish calmness as your baseline state—that is, your normal resting point from which you move into action and to which you naturally return once action is done. This theme is very prominent in Exercise Four.

The best way to teach yourself how to let go of stress and tension is to practice complete relaxation. This also is excellent preparation for hypnosis and self-hypnosis. These reasons are why your first exercise was progressive relaxation. You will continue to find the tape useful to relax yourself whenever you feel particularly tense physically, or if ever you find yourself too mentally worked up to get into the hypnosis.

Mastering relaxation skills has various other strategic benefits in problem solving and self-management. You can remain calm and at ease in the sorts of situations that most used to distress you. You can easily turn off the anxiety, tension, and compulsive feelings so often encountered when dieting, cutting down alcohol, or quitting tobacco.

T. X. Barber suggests as well that relaxation can help you overcome by yourself many phobias or specific fears one might have for situations such as flying in airplanes, being high off the ground, immersing oneself in water, or dealing with strangers. These are just some ways to make use of the fact that *by relaxing yourself, you can control or block unwanted or habitual stress responses such as tension, anxiety, or over-self-consciousness.*

The Practice of Allowing

A close cousin to mastering relaxation skills is a strategy of self-management I call the practice of *allowing.* It seems only practical good sense—but it's something that goes against so much of what we learn growing up as contemporary Americans.

All of us (but boys in particular) were taught that we had to *make* things happen. The way to do this is apply force, effort, strain. You keep on applying brute force until things go the way you want them to go, or until something breaks. One of my students called this the rule of "If it doesn't fit, force it." He relates that he once managed to break a nine-ton vise in this fashion. More commonly, however, it is we ourselves who break.

Reared in a culture telling us never to let go, never to let up, to keep on pushing at things, we are accustomed to keep worrying away at tasks and problems long after we are no longer in any position to actually do something about them. We worry and strain away in our imagination, in our feeling and thinking. That only keeps us tense and uptight.

Behavior therapists, humanistic psychologists, and holistic health practitioners alike urge us to cease and desist from this self-defeating behavior. Usually they advise us to take a passive attitude of the sort advocated by the Oriental philosophies.

Unfortunately, those who tell you to do so don't seem to really understand what Buddhism, Hinduism, or Taoism are really all about; their remarks are way out of context. Such passivism was never intended to be a way of doing things in this world; rather, it is part and parcel of a way of overcoming this world, of striving toward enlightenment. If that is your goal, great. However, passivism doesn't get you far in this or any society—it isn't supposed to. It is not an instrumental way of doing things, but the precise opposite.

As always, though, there is a middle way. This is the way I have called allowing. The idea is this: There are times when you can do something and times when no amount of your effort can have any positive effect. You must learn to discriminate between these two.

When you can act, act—and then relax and cease trying to do anything about it. When you do act, study the situation and select the approach that will use the momentum of events to your best advantage. This will be the easy and effectual way to do it. Learn, in a word, to *nudge* events—don't try to force them.

This means you must both learn to trust your own best judgment and allow things to take their natural course without your constantly intervening. That's how a space probe is sent to distant planets—its course is corrected with a short burst from its engines and then it rides for days, weeks, or months until the next point is reached where a nudge can help. It would never get there by blasting away full steam ahead.

The allowing part seems most difficult to many of us. As you were urged in Exercise Four, you must learn to do what you can do, but then take your mind off that particular project, person, problem, or event, allow yourself to relax and become calm once more, and get on with your life until the next point when you can do something about it.

For example, I meet a woman. I find myself interested, so I conduct myself so as to be favorably thought of while I do what I can to promote a future encounter. Once we part, however, nothing I can do will change anything.

Worrying it over in my imagination won't help. All that does is make me become tense, uptight, anxious, convinced that I'd blown it already. I'd set myself up to get rejected. On the spot, I'd get so nervous and self-conscious my mind would go blank and I'd blow it for sure. I would have been much better off to relax myself with self-hypnosis and stop worrying about it.

You should be ready now to go back over the script for Exercise Four and check out how I incorporated these ideas in your session. For effective self-management and to maximize your performance in any situation, it is wise to follow this rule: *Act, take your mind off the situation or thing, relax, and flow on in your life until the next time comes round when you can really do something about it.* This way you don't block yourself or create unnecessary stress and make things more difficult for yourself. It gives you the best chance to get what you want in the end. What more could you ask for?

Self-Assessment Strategy

Let's get really practical: How do you embark upon your program of self-management training? Well, to begin with, you need a plan of action. Start by assessing the situation.

Let's say I have a lot of books. I need someplace to put them. So I ask myself what it is that I need and how I might satisfy that need. I decide that a bookshelf is the way to go. Then I have to figure out what kind of a bookshelf, sketch it out, and decide what raw materials are needed and what tools will be required to assemble and shape those raw materials into my finished project.

You have the raw materials for your own project—yourself. In this volume, you will find the right tools for most of the jobs you are likely to attempt, as well as directions for modifying these or creating new tools of your own to fit your specific needs.

You have also drawn up a tentative work plan—your self-assessment, done in Exercise Two. At this time, let's consider what went into the exercise; what sort of thinking went into asking those questions you answered.

First, there is a special way of looking at problems. The pragmatic approach is to view what's bugging you as blockages in your living. You find yourself stuck, unable to overcome problems or manage yourself and your life in such a way as to feel your condition is tolerable and your progress toward your goals is acceptable. When you are blocked badly enough, the situation comes to seem intolerable for you.

Perhaps you couldn't manage your calories in such a way as to look and feel the way you crave to be. Perhaps you go blank when taking examinations, or you simply can't maintain the level of motivation and productivity you demand of yourself. Perhaps you are blocked in entirely different ways.

When you feel blocked, you grope for change. How you understand your situation, how self-conscious you are of the problem, what you imagine it is you are looking for, and what you end up doing about it are simply variations in the same basic plot. The story goes like this: You find yourself blocked, so you seek to unblock youself and get back to the business of living your life.

However, there is a science to going about this effectively. It begins with practically assessing the situation you find intolerable. Any problem can be looked at as a situation in which you find yourself blocked, and any such situation presents three separate dimensions.

First, it has a *built-in structure.* You want to look at how the social, material, or economic situation is rigged, how it's put together. Problems very often arise from such built-in factors as your body's health or the working conditions of your job.

Second, look at *what other people are doing.* Others can create all manner of problems you have to deal with. Be particularly concerned about your "significant others," those closest to you or whose actions most influence you on a day-to-day basis. A classic example is the alcoholic spouse.

These two aspects of the total situation are generally beyond your immediate control. With time, finesse, and the right kind of tactics, you might be able to eventually change the situation or get others to change their acts. That doesn't help you on the short term, however.

Fortunately, there is one dimension you can always have some control over—*how you act and react.* You can change how you plug yourself into the situation. You can learn to keep cool and to manage yourself in such a way that you are no longer adversely affected by it. At the very least, you can stop acting in such a way that the situation defeats you.

You don't have to be a victim of circumstances. You don't have to any longer "be yourself," if all that means is you lose again and again. You don't have to let it get to you. You can refuse; you can take control. You are always potentially free. By your actions you can translate that liberty into actuality.

There are two additional, less-obvious principles from Exercise Two or our previous discussion which will prove crucial in turning your assessment into a work plan. The first is recognition of that principle mentioned with regard to the strategic approach generally, *the practical dimensions of your problem*.

What do you get by doing what you have been doing; what are you getting from keeping the situation as a problem to you? For example, the overeater, cigarette smoker, and many other substance abusers reward themselves and manage their stress through an oral habit.

There is a related consideration of equal importance: any unintended by-products of your coping tactics. Look at the possibility that what's bugging you is an unanticipated, long-term effect of the things you've been doing which get you by. The compulsive overeater and the smoker may have to deal, for example, with unacceptable obesity and wrecked lungs, respectively.

When you think about things, remember that you live, feel, suffer, and act in the present. If this helps me cope with right now, that's far more meaningful than what might possibly happen a long time from now. I need it, it helps me, I'll deal with the consequences if they ever become a problem to me.

You don't have to feel guilty if you look at the *practical rationality* of the situation, how your actions serve your actual present-time needs. If there prove to have been undesired longer-term consequences, that's an entirely different matter. You didn't choose to do what you've been doing in order to make yourself miserable sometime in the future. You're not crazy. It's just that there is always a cost to our choices, and some costs prove more intolerable than we had anticipated. That's a mistake, not a personal fault.

The final step is to translate your analysis into a prescription by asking yourself, "What can I do about it?"

Looking over your assessment, what ways can you see to bring about a resolution to the blockages in your life, or at least to make the situation less of a problem for you?

Start by considering how you can affect the problem by changing how you tend to react in such situations. How might you alter your responses or otherwise deal with the others involved or the structure of the situation itself? Are there things you have omitted doing that would resolve the blockage? Do you need to change your own conduct or develop some better strategies that would get you what you want? What else could you possibly do about it?

After brainstorming in this fashion until you run out of new ideas, you should edit your list of alternatives. What possibilities are the most workable, the most appropriate, the most likely to do the most good? Which would be easiest to start with? Now prioritize your list by writing down and numbering the things you can do about it from the most feasible and most important to the least.

Key Technique One: Self-Assessment Strategy
Use

To assess problems and blockages and evaluate what you can do about them.

Method

Pen-and-paper exercise.

Directions

Consider the Seven Assessment Questions, below, to analyze the situation and work out your plan of action. *The Seven Assessment Questions:*

1. What's bugging me?
2. What's going on here? (The action—how does it work, how does the situation hang together? Consider all viewpoints, not just your own.)
3. What part of this situation is built in?
4. What part comes from what other people are doing?

5. What part do I play? (What are you doing or not doing, how are you reacting to contribute to or cause this problem for yourself?)
6. What are its practical dimensions?
7. What can I do about it?

Suggestion:

Go back in your journal now to Exercise Two. Review the questions and how you answered at the time. You may want to modify or redo the entire exercise; at least try to organize a preliminary work plan from those notes.

Doing Something About It

Everything in this volume has been aimed at helping you master new ways of doing something about what bugs you in your life. Let me reinforce something I've been saying all along: Thinking about it is not nor has ever been enough. To change your life you must change what you actually do. You must act, you must do something about it. Nobody else can do what must be done. Only you can.

To most easily and effectually change and successfully manage your life, use your self-interactions to shape and guide what is only natural for you. By changing your realities, as I've discussed, you can steer yourself indirectly and without great effort or need to pay attention to every little detail. The key to all of this is using your imagination strategically.

You can always exercise control over yourself and your situations in your *actions*, your *responses*, and your *attitudes*. That is, you can change what you are inclined to do or how you will tend to react. At a deeper level, you can change your entire orientation toward situations, yourself, or your progress in life by changing how you feel about things and what you expect from them. This is what I mean by your attitudes.

You should never forget that your new realities only will become natural for you, your new ways of living will only become spontaneous and taken for granted by yourself and others to the degree that you enact your new ideas over and over again in the course of living. At first, this will be work. *You will have to make hypnosis work for you by acting as if it's already working—and then it does!*

If my meaning isn't clear, don't worry. You will very shortly discover how that little bit of effort you put into improving yourself in this fashion pays off beyond your wildest expectations. Just remember that you must trigger the process by allowing yourself to act changed.

You can start the change process off even before you actually learn self-hypnosis, in fact. There are a variety of behavioral and visualization tactics you can start off with right now. Some are borrowed from conventional practices; others I've developed myself just as you'll be doing for your own specific case.

If you came to me privately for help with smoking, weight, nail biting or other nervous habits, for help with chronic stress and tension or related problems, here's how we'd begin. First, I'd explain something about strategic hypnosis. Then I'd give you some training in visualization and working with suggestions. Next, I'd give you a progressive-relaxation session and send you home to practice for about a week with a tape virtually identical to yours from Exercise One.

I would also give you some homework to start off with, even before your first hypnosis session.

Key Technique Two: Homework for Nervous Habits
Use
> To begin changing unwanted realities and taking control over your act.

Method
> Read and do as directed.

Directions

Practice any or all of the following as appropriate.

1. Remember that you are not trying not to smoke, snack, drink, or not to indulge in any nervous habit or behavior. Rather, you are going to *allow* yourself not to bother doing those things you no longer wish to be doing. There's an enormous difference.

2. At least for the first week, practice progressive relaxation no less than twice daily, morning and evening.

3. Obtain a small notebook. On the first page, from your self-assessment, list the five areas you are going to work on first. Word each item in terms of what you are going to do about it (e.g., "I refuse to smoke cigarettes under any circumstances," "I can remain calm and relaxed at all times, under any or all circumstances," etc.). Every morning and every evening, review this list. After glancing at each item, repeat it to yourself and then remind yourself why that particular item is so important to you.

4. At least for the first two weeks, use your notebook as a behavioral journal. Jot down any time you find yourself tempted to do what you are now committed to change about yourself or your acts. Note when it was, what was going on, what you did about it. Also write down anything else noteworthy: insights, unusual feelings, things that get to you, etc.

5. Twice daily—at least for the first week, or any time when you feel as if it becomes difficult not to relapse to the old habitual ways—do the following 5 to 10 times in rapid succession:

   A. Pretend you are in a situation in which this is a problem, and feel as if you are about to indulge in the old habit. Really get the feeling of "needing to do it" by imagining you feel this way.

B. Fully consciously, make all the motions of doing that. Playact, but don't actually bite off the fingernail or light and inhale the cigarette, etc. Just make all the motions and feel as if you were doing it.

C. Shut your eyes, take a deep breath, and exhale, saying to yourself, "This is not me. I can relax and enjoy my life. I refuse to—[fill in problem], I'm free!"

D. Open your eyes, relax a moment while feeling the wonderful sensations you can always get when you act in a way that asserts your self-management, and then go back and start again from A.

6. If ever you should still feel really tempted after doing these things, take a sip of cool water and hold off for fifteen minutes. If you still feel a need to give in that cannot be put off any longer, then allow yourself to do so this one time. You'll be surprised how rarely this will be necessary!

Exercise Five: Practicing Behavioral Homework
Purpose

To familiarize yourself with Key Technique Two.

Method

As described. Select any or all of the above tactics as appropriate to your case; modify as necessary to make them fit your particular needs. Skip this exercise if it is inappropriate to your case.

Six

Your
Self-Hypnosis
Routine

You are now ready to begin doing hypnosis with yourself—that's what *self-hypnosis* means. Once you've gotten the hang of thinking, feeling, and imagining along with suggestions, there's nothing especially difficult or tricky about learning to work with suggestions you are giving yourself.

In fact, you've been exposed to a variety of self-hypnosis practices already. What else is listening to a tape recording of your own voice reading a hypnosis script than a form of self-hypnosis? In the future you'll use this same approach from time to time, but with scripts you make up yourself. Unfortunately, this method is impractical for daily use.

You have also been working with a number of *informal self-hypnosis* methods. Also known generically as *suggestion*, such techniques are very often promoted as something other than hypnosis. They are called by more fashionable names such as guided visualization, imagery, biofeedback, meditation, behavior therapy, or affirmations. What they all boil down to is self-hypnosis—thinking, feeling, and imagining along with your own suggestions.

It doesn't matter what you call it, the process is the

same. The only real difference between what you have been doing in most of your experiments and exercises, and what is more commonly thought of as hypnosis or self-hypnosis, is that you just sat down and did them without defining the situation as hypnosis. Hence, I call such methods *informal self-hypnosis.*

Techniques of this kind are relatively loose and un-structured. Normally they begin with relaxing yourself in some way. Then you make up and involve yourself in your imaginations in an open-ended, free-flowing way. Some-times the whole process might take only a few moments to complete; at other times it can go on for as long as you can continue to concentrate.

In self-management, problem solving, and perform-ance enhancement, you will very often find informal tech-niques your method of choice when on the spot, in the actual situation itself. You train yourself to work with them, however, in formal self-hypnosis. You practice them in your imagination, again in formal self-hypnosis. This way, when you need to use them, you will know how to make them work for you. An example of such a tactic is the pause-and-say-zero technique to which you were introduced in Exer-cise Four.

There is, however, no substitute for training yourself to work with a *formal self-hypnosis routine.* In this chapter you will begin working with one. Only by practicing a set routine of this sort can you make the detail work of shifting into use of a hypnotic frame of mind your natural habit. Only by familiarizing yourself with and mastering a standard and unvarying routine can you take your attention off all those little details and focus instead on the actual work you must do in order to achieve your goals.

The discipline of practicing a self-hypnosis ritual is invaluable in and of itself. I cannot stress this too much. If you just take the minimal time and effort required to do your self-hypnosis routine once—or even better, two or three times a day—you will simply amaze yourself. On the other hand, if you don't bother, you will defeat yourself from the very start.

Practicing your self-hypnosis routine no less than daily is the bottom line. Do it and you'll never regret the effort involved. Happily, it's easy to build into the design of your routine all sorts of payoffs and other inducements that make it easy for you to do this. Let's consider a basic self-hypnosis exercise you will be using, and see exactly what is required of you.

Key Technique Three: Basic Self-Hypnosis Routine
Use

To provide an easy and effective way of practicing formal self-hypnosis.

Method

Self-hypnosis (that is, giving yourself suggestions directly and then working with them hypnotically).

Directions

Before you start, always make yourself comfortable, preferably reclining but not flat on your back, in a quiet place where you won't be disturbed for a while. If you are on a tight schedule, set an alarm clock for when you must finish the exercise. Then just follow these steps:

1. Touch a finger to the center of your forehead. Close your eyes and stare at that spot. Return your hand to your side or lap.

2. Take a deep breath and either tense all the muscles of your body at once, or just those of your butt and bottom (if you are already physically loose and relaxed).

3. When you cannot comfortably hold your breath any longer, breathe out as slowly as you possibly can, and at the same time both let your body relax, become limp and loose, and also roll your eyeballs back

down to their normal resting position, as slowly as you can.

4. With the last of your breath as you breathe out, say "zero" to yourself and, as you hear "zero," consciously relax your muscles even more.

5. Now begin repeating "zero" to yourself in your mind, over and over and over. Visualize zeros, imagine hearing the word *zeeerowww*, feel zero, fantasize along with the associations of zero—being empty, a place holder, neither here nor there, neither positive nor negative, a resting place, a hole through which you can escape the objective universe, etc. Saying "zero" just once will calm and clear your mind. Ten or so times will take you deep enough for routine self-hypnosis. The more time you spend saying zero in your imagination, the deeper and more relaxed you will become; 10 to 15 minutes of this will trigger the relaxation response. *You will want to get this deep at least once a day* (the best time is after your day's work is over).

6. When you are ready, give yourself your suggestion. Say the statement out loud, so you can hear yourself saying it. A typical general-purpose suggestion might be "It's good to be alive, I can relax and make things go right for myself—I'm free!"

7. Now repeat your suggestion to yourself for 30 seconds to a minute or so. A good tactic is to imagine it echoing or being sung by a chorus of your inner voices throughout your being, penetrating into every fiber of your body and mind.

8. Then visualize your suggestion, as you will be learning. Use all the senses and all the symbols you can. Take as long as you'd like. When through, it is helpful to imagine the mental picture shrinking into a dot, like the image on a TV set, then vanish into the depths of your mind.

9. Now you can employ any additional hypnotic techniques or practice tactics you are learning.

10. When ready to end your session, repeat your suggestion to yourself, take a deep breath, count up from one to ten, open your eyes, and feel wide awake and get all the pleasurable sensations you'll always feel upon completing a session of hypnosis or self-hypnosis. *Be sure to let yourself feel these good feelings*; they are very important.

Experiment Twelve: What Is Self-Hypnosis Like?

Purpose

To experience how the above routine works.

Method

Guided fantasy. Tape-record and work with a session script.

Directions

You are going to have yourself imagine doing self-hypnosis, but not actually do it this time. Prepare your tape and then just listen to it, imagining along with your voice.

Script

"I am going to let myself experience how it will be to do my basic self-hypnosis routine. As I begin, I am letting myself begin to relax so I can really concentrate and follow along with my directions.

"One. I will actually touch my finger to the center of my forehead to start the process. I do this now, and roll up my eyes as I would do by myself, in self-hypnosis.

"Two. I actually take a deep breath and really tense all my muscles at once, just as I've been doing in progressive relaxation, but all at once. (Pause 10 seconds.)

"Three. When I can't hold my breath any longer, I breathe out as slowly as I can, letting go in my body and mind, rolling my eyes back down to their normal, relaxed position as slowly as I am able. I let myself actually do this now. . . . (10-second pause.)

"Four. As I breathe out the last of my breath, I imagine saying 'zero' to myself once, and I imagine becoming totally limp and loose in my body when I hear myself saying 'zero' this first time. I continue breathing at my own natural rate for the rest of this session.

"Five. I imagine thinking and feeling and picturing zero now, over and over in my mind . . . one zero makes me feel calm and clear and relaxed . . . not at all hypnotized . . . balanced perfectly . . . but as I keep on thinking and imagining zero, I slip deeper and deeper, faster and faster, more and more naturally into a deep hypnotic frame of mind . . . becoming more and more relaxed as I think and picture zero . . . saying zero for half a minute relaxes me completely . . . each additional time sends me deeper and deeper . . . if I also squeeze my eyes and relax them a few times while I imagine zero, I can go more easily deeper still . . . saying and picturing zeros . . . little zeros and big zeros . . . fat zeros and skinny zeros . . . short funny zeros and tall happy zeros . . . zeros every color of the rainbow . . . the sound of zero . . . the feeling of zero . . . slipping out through the hole in the zero and leaving reality behind for a while . . . feeling more and more zero . . . like a place holder . . . neither here nor there . . . neither positive nor negative . . . peaceful . . . perfect calmness with me around it . . . as clear and still as a diamond . . . zero . . . zero . . . a wonderful feeling of peace and freedom and warmth and safety . . . zero . . . saying and thinking zero like this for fifteen minutes or so gives me the relaxation response . . . it feels so good I want to do this every day . . . to just let go completely . . . perfect peace and comfort . . . letting all the pressure out . . . so good . . . relaxing like this after the day's work is over lets me feel good and really enjoy my hard-earned leisure time . . . more and more every day . . . I can enjoy just relaxing like this and doing nothing at all . . . and I find myself more and more enjoying doing all sorts of other things in my spare time also . . . whatever I'd like to do . . . trying new things, new activities . . . just being the sort of person I have always wanted to be . . . zero . . . zero . . . it's so good . . . soooo goood . . . even ten zeros and I'm there . . . where I want to be in order to make my suggestions and visualization really do what I want them to do for me . . . I will always know when I'm deep enough, because I'll feel it, I'll just *know* . . . because I can really and truly trust myself now . . . more and more . . . zero . . . .

"Six. Now I give myself a suggestion when I do self-hypnosis . . . I'll just imagine myself doing it this time . . . imagine myself whispering out loud a suggestion like, 'It's good to be alive, I can relax and make things go right for myself—I'm free!'

"Seven. Now I imagine repeating that suggestion to myself over and over in my mind . . . feeling even more than hearing it echoing all the way through even the deepest levels of my mind . . . as if a chorus of angelic voices was singing it inside me . . . reverberating through every strand and fiber, every nook and cranny of my being . . . 'It's good to be alive . . . I can relax and make things go right for myself . . . I'm free!' (10-second pause.)

"Eight. Here's where I visualize myself being and feeling and acting naturally the way I have suggested to myself . . . I imagine myself being, feeling, and acting free . . . free to make things go right for myself . . . free of anything or everything that could hold me back . . . free of frustrations and problems and blockages . . . really feeling it is good to be alive . . . let me see what sort of visualization comes into my mind this time . . . I'll just let myself do whatever comes into my mind now when I think of being free, of making my life work out right . . . [30-second pause] . . . now I let this imaginary reality collapse and shrink into a tiny dot of light and vanish somewhere deep into my mind, where it can work itself into my deepest thinking and feeling. . . .

"Nine. This is where I can work with my self-hypnosis techniques and train myself in the informal tactics I can learn to work with outside hypnosis when on the spot. . . .

"Ten. This is where I count myself up, out of my session . . . however, this time, I will only imagine doing so . . . I imagine I say my suggestion to myself again, 'It's good to be alive, I can relax and make things go right for myself—I'm free!' . . . and I imagine then taking a deep breath, counting from one to ten, opening my eyes, and really feeling just great, wide awake, refreshed, relaxed and wonderful . . . really feeling the beneficial effects of my session . . . and feeling also those strong pleasure feelings flooding through my body and mind that I always feel when completing a session of hypnosis, when I've used one of my techniques, or when I've done anything else to assert my freedom and my self-control . . . but now, I just let myself relax for a few more minutes and allow the certainty that I can and that I will be able to do self-hypnosis successfully, easily, and with great benefit grow deeper and deeper into my mind . . . I feel I want to do it every day . . . that I will let nothing stop me because this is something I am doing for myself . . . [5-second pause] . . . and now, I actually do take a deep breath, count from one to ten, and feel exactly as I've imagined feeling after my sessions . . . [15-second pause] . . . wide awake, feeling *wonderful!*"

End of script. After your session, note how it went, how you are feeling, and anything else worth recording. Do not save this tape, however; you want to learn how to do it on your own.

It's as easy as that to do. Unfortunately, developing a workable self-hypnosis technique can be something of a chore. At least it was when I began working in this field; nobody seemed to think it worth bothering to explain the practical logic involved. I had to work this out for myself in five years' clinical practice. Now I can explain to you not only what to do, but how to build a self-hypnosis exercise.

By studying this logic, you can both help yourself work with self-hypnosis to your greatest benefit, and you can see how to modify the basic technique or eventually develop one of your own to better fit your own unique needs. The only claims I make for this basic technique are that it is easily learned, easy to do, works well, and can be easily adapted to the greatest possible variety of uses. Let us, therefore, look at what goes into this routine.

First, it has a beginning and an end. This fact is really quite important. By clearly defining when you begin and end your session, you do several things. You make it clear to yourself that your hypnosis is only a temporary state of affairs, that you will return to "normal," so you don't have to worry. In fact, it clearly shows you how to bring yourself back.

Although in fact you can just snap back into everyday functioning at will, a ritual like this gives you something to rely on. That's why your standard routine is so very important. It gives you clear and unmistakable milestones telling you for sure where you are now, where you've been, and what comes next. These will always be there for you to hold on to, so you can relax, let go, turn your back on reality for a while, and have no fear of somehow getting lost inside yourself.

By ritualizing this whole process, you make it safe for yourself. It gives you something known to always rely on. It ensures that you will be able to return; it gives you control over what happens to you. It is not necessary, but I cannot overemphasize how much it can help you.

This is the reason I've taught you all along that you can at any time bring yourself out of session by just taking a new breath, counting from one to ten, and opening your eyes. To your self-hypnosis we add the step of repeating your suggestion; this will keep it on your mind as you return to normalcy.

The awakening procedure is similar to others used by nearly all hypnosis practitioners. Its primary function is to serve as a cue to yourself, signaling that you are leaving hypnosis and resuming normal, reality-based functioning. Technically, the deep breath makes a pause in the ongoing action and creates physical sensations providing a cue on the feeling level. Counting up provides a gradual, clearly marked transition, while giving you the sense of returning from deep within. Opening your eyes restores the visual cues by which you anchor yourself in the environment, telling you where you are located in space and time.

This touches upon a second important point: *Always couple verbal definition of the situation or promptings to do or experience something with physical actions that will add a clear feeling component.* This is one of the unspoken secrets of effective hypnosis. It both adds the sense of reality to your statements and eases the process of routinizing hypnotic tactics—making actions or procedures your habit, so you don't have to consciously attend to or think about them. By using this trick, you set yourself up to respond spontaneously to your own cues.

If you are wise, you'll select behaviors that are easy to associate with the meanings you want to give things, or with the events you wish to prompt. Consider the very first step in your basic self-hypnosis routine.

Experiment Thirteen: That "Trancy" Feeling

Purpose

To explore how you feel when you do different things with your eyeballs.

Method

Read and do. No need to tape.

Directions

First, just close your eyes and do nothing for a few moments. As you sit there, pay attention to any sensations you can feel and any changes you can notice in your physical state or subjective awareness. Open your eyes.

Second, as in your routine, touch an index finger to the center of your forehead—this is the mystical "third eye" of the yogis. Roll your eyes up and in to stare at that spot, and hold them there for a few moments. As before, observe any changes or sensations. Then open and relax your eyes.

Third, squeeze your eyes tightly shut for a few moments. Observe. Now squeeze and relax them, squeeze and relax again and again for a minute or so. How does that affect you?

Now open your eyes and make some notes in your journal concerning the different effects and sensations (if any) you experienced from the different procedures. Can you see why I selected one or another procedure for specific hypnosis and self-hypnosis exercises? What sorts of events, interpretations, or behaviors are best facilitated by each of these three ways of manipulating your eyeballs?

T. X. Barber describes the sensations you get from rolling up your eyes or staring at the center of your forehead as a "trancy feeling." It is very easy to imagine you are entering an altered state of consciousness when you are already feeling this way.

I selected touching your forehead as the opening step of your self-hypnosis routine for another reason as well. It clearly defines the start of your session; when you do this, you can tell you are about to do self-hypnosis, you can *feel* it. Since there are almost no other times you would do anything like this, it provides a clear and unmistakable cue defining what occurs between then and when you perform the equally unlikely actions of ending your session as "hypnosis."

It would be silly to use something ordinary for this purpose. There's no reason you couldn't start the session by just closing your eyes—but how does that differentiate this from other times you close your eyes in daily life? Opening your eyes, on the other hand, is a perfect choice for "awakening." In that case, the fact that this is something you do in the course of daily life works to its advantage.

However, there is no reason why squeezing and relaxing your eyes wouldn't work well for starting the session. It certainly produces a clear and unmistakable feeling component. Since rolling up the eyes was already in common use in starting hypnosis, I decided to follow precedent—later I realized why that particular action fit so well in that particular application. Experimentation indicated to me that the eye-squeezing technique would serve even better to symbolize going deeper, since it made your eyes so tired they just didn't want to move. That's why I've had you use it for this purpose rather than another.

The Induction of Self-Hypnosis

It is not in any way necessary to incorporate a special starting cue in the self-hypnosis procedure. You could just begin with a relaxation exercise, or even go directly to a visualization. In my practice I might select one or the other of these alternatives for selected clients. However, on the whole and for myself I prefer to incorporate a clear and unambiguous action with a strong feeling component to signal start of hypnosis.

The part of any session in which you establish the situation and frame of mind we identify as hypnosis is usually called the *induction*. Parts two through five of your routine serve this purpose. They represent a combination of relaxation techniques gleaned from many sources. These include a form of progressive relaxation, deep breathing, letting the eyes roll *down* (using their downward motion as a symbolic suggestion, combined with the sensations of releasing strain), using zero as a verbal cue to relax, which is then further utilized as both a symbol and a sort of mantra or relaxation-response device to be repeated over and over. These steps cover the gamut of commonly used relaxation techniques.

There are other ways of entering hypnosis. Two that I have found useful at times are imagining yourself getting wider and wider awake, or getting higher and higher in any way you'd care to interpret that phrase. However, strategically, it pays off to fit deep relaxation in somewhere along the line, since you'll want to obtain the benefits of deep psychosomatic relaxation. Therefore, it never hurts to follow the principle that *it is always a good idea to get yourself deeply relaxed to facilitate entering a hypnotic frame of mind.*

If you'd like, there are two further relaxation techniques worth exploring for use with self-hypnosis. One is to employ massage as a way of relaxing your body, and then to go on to your imagining work. This requires finding a cooperative massage partner, but it may just do the trick if you have real difficulties letting your body relax completely. Even if this is not a problem for you, massage is something you might want to play with.

Second, many clients who initially found it difficult to get into their self-hypnosis overcame that difficulty by doing their exercise while soaking in a warm bath. You might want to try this, or just experiment for fun with doing your self-hypnosis in a bath or hot tub. Obviously, however, this tactic is limited with respect to where and when you can use it.

The basic exercise gives you complete discretion with regard to how long or how deep to go. This is a particular benefit of using a repetitive technique; it enormously expands your options. You can use the same procedure of saying zero to clear your mind, get into session, deepen your hypnosis, or trigger the relaxation response. By the amount of time you spend saying zero to yourself, you can create the precise effect you want at the time.

To get the full benefit from this technique, you must do more than just say the phrase over and over. You have to involve both your thinking and your feeling as fully as possible. This is why I have instructed you to say, hear, and visualize zero. You want to be able to almost *feel* it. One very enjoyable and highly effective way to bring about this holistic involvement is to use fantasy, particularly cartoon images. This tactic is not only fun to do, keeping you interested and involved, but it also permits you to choose symbolism reminding you of the feelings and effects you wish to bring about for yourself. Look back over Experiment Eleven to see how this can be done.

SEVEN

Making Self-Hypnosis Work for You

Once you have gotten yourself relaxed and into a hypnotic frame of mind, you are ready to make self-hypnosis work for you. This part of the session you are entering, often called the body of the session, is where most of the important action takes place in strategic self-hypnosis—the actual work of reconstructing your realities.

Although there are rare times when you might want to skip this step, you will always want to begin the body of your session with what I have been calling your suggestion. In Experiment Twelve, for example, you used the statement, "It's good to be alive, I can relax and make things go right for myself—I'm free!"

This is a different way of using verbal suggestion than those discussed in your previous chapter. Sometimes referred to as an affirmation, this kind of suggestion serves as a verbal formula expressing what you want to get out of your self-hypnosis.

In selecting your self-hypnosis suggestion, affirmation, or formula, it is wise to follow one of the unspoken tricks of the hypnotist's trade: *Always make what you do serve as many purposes as possible.* In this way, you get the most payoff from the least amount of effort. Therefore, you want to phrase this statement in the most general or most easily generalizable terms possible; that is, you want to select a formula that you can feel relates both to your immediate or specific goals and to your overall self-management objectives.

Typically, the formulas you will use in strategic self-hypnosis will be directed primarily at your *attitudes* or your *conduct.* The suggestion we have been using as our example is of the attitude kind. It suggests an orientation toward yourself, your life circumstances, or your action—a way of looking at events, circumstances, and feelings that gives you power over them.

Conduct suggestions define and prompt what you will do. In this regard, remember that *not* doing, blocking action, and particularly *refusing to do, feel, need, or want* are all actions you can take. These are extremely potent approaches to changing long-standing habit patterns, where your first objective must be to cease doing that which is messing up your life.

As a rule, I urge you to *always combine conduct suggestions with attitude statements promoting self-management.* It is almost always appropriate to at least add to your statement the words, "I'm free!" These convey both the sense of freedom from having to do or not do anything—freedom from stress, disabilities, blockages, or other negative conditions; and that of freedom to be, do, think, and feel as you yourself choose.

Rather than go into further detail, let's consider some examples my students and clients have found especially useful.

Key Technique Four: Self-Hypnosis "Formulas"
Use
> To define what the new reality is that you are creating for yourself through self-hypnosis.

Method
> Done per instructions for your basic routine.

Examples

  A. For General Self-Management.

    1. "It's good to be alive, I'm free!"
    2. "It's okay . . . I can do it, I'm free!"
    3. "I can relax and enjoy my life now, I'm free!"
    4. "I can relax and enjoy my life and make things go right for myself—I'm free!"
    5. "I can relax and get my life together, making things go right for myself—I'm free!"
    6. "It's good to be alive. I can relax and make things go right for myself—I'm free!"

  B. For Stress Management and Relaxation.

    7. "I can remain calm and relaxed under any or all circumstances. I'm free."
    8. "I will cope with each thing as it comes up, to the best of my ability, and then continue, still calm and relaxed. I'm free."
    9. "I will be relaxed and enjoy my life—I'm free!"

  C. Changing Habits.

    10. "I will feel relaxed and I will be strong. I refuse to overeat and make myself fat—I'm free!"
    11. "I will feel relaxed and I will be strong. I am not a smoker. I will not place cigarettes or anything in place of cigarettes into my mouth because I don't want to—and not smoking will make me feel good."
    12. "I can enjoy my life. I can relax and refuse to need tobacco or anything in place of tobacco. I'm free!"
    13. "I will be relaxed and I will be strong. I refuse to need alcohol or get myself drunk. I'm free!"

  D. Improving Performances.

    14. "I will feel relaxed and I will be strong. I will feel good about myself and assert myself when and how I feel I should. I'm free!"
    15. "Because I am relaxed and because I am strong, I

will focus my full attention on everything I need to concentrate on, and when I am put to the test, my mind will remain calm and clear and I will remember everything I need to know. I can do it—I'm free!"

16. "I can relax and enjoy my life and do what I feel I should do, when I feel I should do it. I'm free!"

17. "I can relax and feel confident and allow myself to do my very best in all situations and in everything I do. I'm free!"

18. "I will feel calm and relaxed under all circumstances, I will be strong, and I will feel a tremendous and intense concentration power with everything I do."

19. "I will feel relaxed and I will be strong. I will be fast, accurate, and successful in court reporting. I'm free."

20. "I can relax and enjoy feeling myself typing each new word as I hear [or see] it, quickly, accurately, and correctly. Nothing can stop me—I'm free!"

Further Tips:

1. When you are seeking to overcome and resist temptations, it is wise to include a phrase like "and I will be strong."

2. If what you are seeking to do has been impossible or extraordinarily difficult for you in the past, or you have never experienced anything other than having the problem (such as an obese person who has never been slender), add a "more and more" formula. For example, "I can feel more and more relaxed under pressure each and every new day, because I am not a robot—I'm free!"

3. Particularly if you have a prior history of straining and failing at stress-related goals such as losing weight, quitting tobacco, or cutting down drinking,

you should use a feeling cue in your suggestion. For example, when you say your formula out loud, do it like this: "I will feel relaxed [exhale] and I will be strong. . . ."

Exercise Six: Selecting Your Personal Formula

Purpose

To select a suggestion with which to begin working in your self-hypnosis routine.

Method

Pen-and-paper exercise.

Directions

First, review the entire portion of this chapter under the heading "Giving Yourself the Suggestion." Then go over Key Technique Four carefully, examining the list of examples and observing how they are put together.

Now turn back in your journal to your most recent self-assessment. Is there a common theme to the goals you are working toward or the things you are trying to change about yourself or your life? If not, what is your first priority—what goals or attitudes do you wish to work on first? (Almost always you'll find the first case to be your own, with your goals and problems focused around a similar theme such as getting nervous under pressure, feeling uptight, needing to relax and concentrate, etc.)

Is there a suggestion on the list of examples that fits this need as is? Can you slightly modify one to fit your case more exactly? Otherwise, follow the principles we've been discussing and make up one of your very own. *Note: Never use directly or indirectly negative suggestions.* For example, if you want to lose weight, *don't* tell yourself, "I will stick to my prescribed diet and when I have eaten all that I am supposed to eat, I will no longer be hungry." Not only are you inviting yourself to resist what you are "supposed to do," but why are you implying that you might feel hungry? Rather, look at number 10 in the Key Technique above. I've used this with over a hundred cases to great success—can you see how it is, indeed, an affirmation, a positive suggestion? (To refuse is, as I've explained, positive—something you *can* do.) Beware also of making your suggestion feel like a matter of work or of taking orders. Keep it positive, feeling like something you would want to do.

The formula should be no more than a few phrases long. The one exception I normally make to this rule is with suggestions for memory, study, or concentration (see number 15). Play with your formula and its wording until it feels right to you. Then write it down in your journal with a big box around it, or do it in colored ink, so you can easily find it later. (Feel free to change or modify your formula at any time, understanding, of course, that you need to give yourself a chance to see how it works for you before you drop it for something else entirely.)

When to Choose a New Formula. So long as you feel comfortable with the formula you have selected, give it a chance to work. How long? A reasonable period of time—at least a couple of weeks. If you feel some progress toward your goals, stick with it until (a) you feel you are well on your way to spontaneously doing as you wanted to be doing and it is no longer a problem for you, or (b) if a very long while has gone by with no appreciable change or progress. In the first case, either select a new suggestion working toward other areas in your self-assessment, or switch to a more general self-management formula. In the second case, either change suggestions and give the new one a few weeks to work, select a different area to work on, or consult a professional for assistance.

As discussed in Chapter Two, you are telling yourself what to believe and what to do twenty-four hours a day. In strategic hypnosis, you work to gain voluntary control over this process of giving yourself suggestions in your subconscious thinking. To create new personal realities, you need to change what you are telling yourself all the time—in effect, you want to change the internal "tape recordings."

You can do so by taking advantage of the principle of repetition. By repeating your new ideas for yourself over and over, they become familiar to you. The more familiar they are, the easier it will be to just take them for granted as your reality. Before long you will find yourself spontaneously reminding yourself of these things as part of your background thinking.

Never underestimate the vast potential inherent in changing your automatic thinking. You generally find yourself doing what seems "only natural" for you to do next. This includes how you feel—you tend to feel the way your thinking suggests.

The reverse of this is also true. You tend to avoid doing or not allow yourself to do what seems unrealistic or unimaginable for you. By changing the realities you define for yourself in your spontaneous background thinking, you enable yourself to overcome self-imposed blocks and disabilities, to unblock hidden or repressed potentialities, and make it possible to explore new ways of being yourself. In this fashion, you can use your thinking strategically to expand the range of your skills, roles, and performances in life.

What's possible by this device? Just ask yourself this question: *What could you conceivably do, experience, have, accomplish, or be if only you could let yourself function to your fullest potential?* Any of these things can be yours if you're willing to put in the necessary work to accomplish that objective.

In order to drive your new ideas expressed by the formula you have selected into your background thinking, you use repetition. After you say your suggestion that first time to yourself, you want to repeat it over and over in your mind for a while. This, along with that final repetition as you end your session, helps you internalize these new realities. By regular practice of these techniques, it can happen for you exactly as you've been hoping.

Two tips can facilitate your success in this task. The first is to imagine along with your thinking, as was suggested in your exercise. The other is applicable if your suggestion is a very long one, or if you are primarily working on your attitudes. In either of these two cases, you might like to use this shortcut: Just repeat to yourself the words "I'm free!" *This will work for any suggestion so long as you make it clear to yourself as you begin what you mean by "I'm free!"* That is, let these words mean what you are telling yourself by your formula, as well as anything else you'd like them to mean for you.

Visualizing the Suggestion

Your verbal formula sets the stage and the scene. Now you create a full-blown fantasy on that theme.

Old-fashioned hypnotists relied on verbal suggestion alone. Modern behavior therapists often skip the suggestion entirely. I've experimented with both approaches, but have always ended up concluding that *thinking and feeling have a synergistic relationship—that is, when you work with both together, you become free to work at your highest potential.*

There is no reason not to use both, and every reason to do so. As I've already discussed the principle of how to do visualization, let's consider instead how to work with your imagining in part seven of your self-hypnosis routine.

At the outset, let's make one point clear. There is a difference between what is suitable when working with a taped script or another person taking the hypnotist role, and when working by yourself in self-hypnosis. In the first case we generally define the meaning of the situation verbally. This is inappropriate, by and large, in the second case of working by yourself without a tape.

To verbally comment upon your experiences requires stepping outside of them, breaking the flow of imagining to disengage yourself enough to think and talk about it. This can shatter the sense of realism you have worked so hard to build up for yourself. Instead, therefore, *to maximize the benefits from your self-hypnosis visualizations, rely on symbolic or other nonverbal ways of defining the meaning of the situation.*

You have already practiced steering your imagination in this indirect fashion by filling the visualization with symbols, props, images, decorations, and other sensory contents meaningful to yourself (if to nobody else). This tactic allows you to define the situation by the context you imagine for it, and by envisioning things or experiences that communicate to you what the imaginary situation is, what it means for you, and what it feels like to you. That takes the place of telling yourself these things. Take advantage of this tactic—it will serve you well.

For self-management and problem solving, you can use any of three related strategies of visualization. The first method is the least directive. You tell yourself your formula and then you just let yourself fantasize—feel and imagine—along with that theme in an unstructured, easy, and playful way. This is most appropriate when you have no particular problem or specific objective on your mind, when you are working toward general or longer-term self-management goals, or if you have found yourself blocked, frustrated, and unable to find a way to deal satisfactorily with a problematic situation. We can call this approach *drifting along with your suggestion.*

Since it's far easier to do than to explain, let's experiment.

Experiment Fourteen: Drifting Along With Suggestions
Purpose
To explore this simplest method of visualization.

Method

Read and do, no need to tape.

Directions

Consider this affirmation: *"I can enjoy and wonderfully benefit from doing my self-hypnosis at least once or twice a day."* Read it out loud a few times, until you can say it to yourself without looking at this book.

Close your eyes. Take a deep breath and tense all the muscles of your butt and bottom. Relax and breathe out as slowly as you can. Now say the formula to yourself out loud once. Then repeat it a few times in your mind, and begin to let yourself daydream along with it. Perhaps start off by narrating to yourself in your thoughts how you are practicing your routine self-hypnosis, really getting into it, saying the suggestion to yourself, and . . . Guide yourself consciously up to "and," then let your mind drift. Let whatever will come into your mind come, and allow your fantasy to flow naturally, however it wants. Don't bother to try directing it. (This is a trick I and many people use to fall asleep—construct a sexual or other wish-fulfillment fantasy and then just let our mind wander as it will.) Go on for as long as you'd like, then take a deep breath, count up, and end the experiment by opening your eyes.

Do this a few times until you get the hang of letting your mind wander along a suggested theme. Make notes in your journal regarding any difficulties, especial successes, or interesting experiences. Try to write out what works best for you.

The second method is more directive. This involves imagining yourself easily and naturally doing as your formula suggests. A person who wishes to quit smoking cigarettes, for example, might picture him- or herself feeling calmly relaxed, perhaps in a setting where it used to be very difficult not to smoke—such as a bar, or while drinking the morning's first cup of coffee—and, in that scene, just matter-of-factly turning down a chance to have a cigarette. *Always follow the visualization of yourself carrying out your suggestion with imagining how good it makes you feel to do so.*

A student with an upcoming final exam might, alternatively, visualize actually taking the test exactly the way he or she would want to handle the exam. In this visualization, one should be certain to imagine feeling the feelings they want to feel in that situation; to notice how clearly their mind thinks, recalls, and otherwise functions when in the test situation; and to feel the positive feelings they will get when they actually find themselves "acing" the exam, knowing they have done well.

This tactic might be labeled *visualizing the suggestion coming true.* It's done identically to the visualization you performed in previous chapters, except that you are guiding yourself along the specific theme of your formula.

Remembering the Future

Our third and final strategy is the most sophisticated and will, therefore, be explained in greater detail. This method, called *remembering the future,* is especially important to master because it represents your basic strategy for self-management training. With this technique you can edit and revise, so to speak, your sense of what script you will be acting out in your life.

To do this, by using your self-hypnosis skills, you visualize the future you wish for yourself as if it were already so. You imagine remembering how it went for you, how it all worked out. The idea is to *create a vision of your own future that becomes a self-fulfilling prophecy.*

By visualizing this way again and again, your ideas lose their "as if" quality—you seem to be seeing the actual future. Here, too, you are making the principle of repetition work for you. You become so familiar with seeing, feeling, and imagining yourself acting as if these things were already objective fact that you begin to take them for granted. You are actually *rehearsing in your imagination*. Over time, your new realities seem to be inevitable, something there would be no way to avoid even if you so desired. You begin to find yourself behaving as if what you are visualizing were something you remembered had already occurred.

In remembering the future, keep in mind that there are no rules governing your imaginations. They are not bound by reality in any way. You can visualize a completely realistic experience, but you could also work with a surreal fantasy or even a cartoon. You can visualize the same future differently each time, if you'd like, so long as you stick to your basic theme. About the worst thing you could do, on the other hand, is to bore yourself into apathy—so *be creative and make it fun to play with your mind.*

Remembering the future is easiest in conjunction with a verbal formula. Give yourself the suggestion and then illustrate its themes for yourself in any way you choose, realistic or fantastic. A simple tactic is to imagine yourself very old, leafing through a scrapbook filled with snapshots, documents, news clippings, and other memorabilia. You might also have yourself reading an old and faded diary, or watching a documentary film.

Whatever you do, bring your suggestion to vivid life. You want to experience the ideas contained in your formula as accomplished, actual facts, or to experience the sort of events and situations that symbolize your having already made these ideas into realities.

A student of mine recently said she had for a long time symbolized her success by imagining a yacht she dreams of possessing. She has actually looked at boats and daydreamed about the kind of vessel she'll eventually purchase. It will be a thirty-foot, two-masted sailboat painted white with red trim. In her visualizations, she begins by picturing herself sailing out past San Francisco's Golden Gate Bridge on a six-week cruise up the Pacific Coast. Once she gets that in her mind, she imagines remembering back to accomplishing her financial goals one by one. This fits well with her formula, "I can relax and enjoy making things go right for myself. I'm free!"

To organize your future memory work, you might want to differentiate different kinds of self-management goals. Each goes best with a different approach to visualizing the future. Let's consider four common variations.

Sometimes your interest is simply a *new attitude and way of living*. Often it is to learn how to remain calm, relaxed, and in control over your life. Something surreal might be appropriate—even something as indirect as picturing yourself as an eagle lazily soaring among the fluffy white clouds, high up in the cool mountain air. More practical-minded persons might prefer visualizing themselves in what would have previously been a very difficult situation, the kind that always used to get to them—but now remembering how self-hypnosis changed all that for them, how easily they learned to manage situations of that type, how well they have come to bring it off for themselves.

Instead, you might be interested in *specific career goals*. Let's say you wanted to become a stage actress. You might picture yourself remembering the opening night of your Broadway debut as a leading lady . . . the third encore, holding a huge bouquet of flowers, the audience on its feet roaring acclaim, your fellow actors beaming and hugging you. Just put in all the details that would belong in such a scene, plus all the extras you'd like.

In the third case, you might want to focus on *mastering the final steps to your success*. If you were a law student seeking to improve your study and memorization skills, you could begin by imagining that you have just opened the letter notifying you of passing the bar—your mind flashes back to when you sat down to the exam . . . how you felt so calm, alert, ready to perform at your very best . . . and how you did so. You remember setting your mind and then carefully reading the first question, quickly and accurately seeing exactly what is written there, exactly what is being asked. You imagine remembering how your mind squeezed itself like a sponge, so that all the facts and know-how were right there for you . . . how you calmly, surely, and in professional, lawyerlike fashion wrote the answer to that first question . . . and then, still calm and relaxed, went on to the next question in the same way. You remember that, before you knew it, you had answered the last question of the bar exam, knowing that you had done well. Imagine feeling at the time that you just knew you had done your very best and had passed the bar.

In the fourth case, you are working on the idea of enacting a whole new reality for yourself. If you were seeking once and for all to overcome a weight problem, I'd suggest you imagine something like this: You are at a party. It's summer, pleasantly warm. You notice a swimming pool off to your left, bright blue in the sunlight. You smell barbecues going, and you notice a line of picnic tables before you, on which is heaped every food you ever craved. You notice that you hold a plate in your hand, and that on the plate there is *one taste* of practically everything there is to eat. The only thing you've taken lots of is the green salad, without much dressing.

You imagine somebody offering you another helping of cake. You smile and tell them, "Thanks, but I've already had enough—it's simply *delicious.*" You know they had made the cake especially for you, and this makes them feel really proud.

Now you notice you are wearing a bathing suit. Assuming that you are a woman, you notice that it's a teeny two-piece bikini of the sort you always wished you could fit into. And you realize you've had this suit for years. Tell yourself it's a size five (or whatever you want to fit into). Admire your suit.

Then you imagine going to the poolside, really smug

about the looks you're getting—particularly the envious looks from some of the chubbier women, who are gobbling down their food as if they couldn't stop eating. You perform a racing dive . . . feeling so healthy and graceful, proud of yourself and of your body . . .

In short, you describe to yourself your new future reality as if it were something unremarkable. You choose to "remember" a slice of life. It may help to add to the picture, as above, images of others who are behaving the way you feel you once did. This symbolizes how much you've changed.

How, then, do you actually do future remembering?

Key Technique Five: Remembering the Future

Use

To visualize your formula or as a self-management strategy in part nine of the self-hypnosis routine.

Method

Self-guided visualization.

Directions

Give yourself your suggestion and repeat it in your mind, or just tell yourself what your goals or objectives will be. Then intentionally construct a fantasy experience as if you were in the distant future remembering back to how and when you succeeded in attaining your purposes. If using a surrealistic visualization, all this can be implied by the imagery itself. There is no fixed rule about how long to spend or how extensive the future memory should be; rather, follow the principle: *Do what feels right.*

Follow the identical principle when it comes to selecting the actual method, content, and duration of the visualization. *There is really no way to do it wrong, so trust yourself.* If you don't like the way it goes this time, do something else next session.

Don't, however, forget to organize your future

memory along the theme of what you want to be, do, or have happen in your life. You may include things above and beyond your actual suggestion. Just keep it appropriate and you'll do fine: *Make the whole thing tell you that you have really brought off what you are seeking to bring about for yourself.*

It is always wise to incorporate general symbolism and other content relating generally to the idea of effective self-management: *Have your future memories show you that you are truly free, unself-consciously in control over yourself and your life, and that being calm and relaxed is your natural state.* The idea that your hands are warm, steady, and relaxed suggests, for example, that you are not tense or nervous.

Make a point of decorating your visualization with details symbolizing what you wish to have attained in life. Think in terms of furnishings, appliances, other artifacts, your and other people's clothing and appearance, the location of the scene, who belongs in this picture with you, what they are doing or saying. Little details are most important, but also try luxury items, yachts and fancy homes or sports cars, an office setting of high prestige, diplomas on the wall, etc.

In all cases, keep it interesting to yourself. You can vary the details of what you imagine each time you do remembering the future. It is essential that you do not create monotony or boredom for yourself. Therefore, make it a point to *let your self-hypnosis work be fun, a form of play.*

Experiment Fifteen: Remembering the Future
Purpose
> To see how you can create future visualizations to facilitate your self-management goals.

Method
> Tape and imagine along as directed.

Directions

Go back to your self-assessment once again and review your self-management goals. Now think for a few moments of how you might include all or most of them in a future visualization following the principles described in Key Technique Five and the examples immediately preceding it. Review that material if you'd like.

Don't worry about doing it "right," just select whatever feels interesting and worth trying. You don't need an actual script, but you might wish to jot down some notes reminding you of what you want to have in your memory.

Tape as follows: First, tell yourself to relax, close your eyes, take a deep breath, and say "zero" as you breathe out, allowing yourself to relax. Now just describe your future memory to yourself, out loud.

Play your tape and imagine along with your suggestions. Your tape should be about 3 minutes long. When it's through, open your eyes and think over what worked well, what needs to be changed, what else you might want to add to really do it right.

Make some notes for an improved tape, and record over the last suggestions, using your new ideas. This tape should also be no longer than about 3 minutes long. Remember to approach this experiment as a form of play and to have fun with it. Listen to this tape and see how it goes. Keep listening and retaping until you feel pretty good about it.

Now take that deep breath and count yourself up. Make some notes in your journal—particularly about any especially good ideas, images, symbols, or tricks you've discovered for yourself.

After your basic visualization in part eight of the basic routine, you can do additional work remembering the future with regard to other goals or anything else you are learning to do in self-hypnosis. When you're done with part nine, end your session as instructed.

A Sneaky Trick

One last point about future memories and other hypnotic work. From the perspective of this present moment, the future is only an idea. It has no behavioral, cognitive, or sensory reality. If you must wait for the future before getting anything out of what you are doing, you will most likely wander off track, lose motivation and interest, become distracted, and never get anywhere at all.

Why do that to yourself? Instead, set yourself up to win by always giving yourself an *immediate payoff* rewarding you for every positive step or action you take toward your goals. This is the practical wisdom behind **B. F.** Skinner's operant conditioning method. You might agree or disagree with his theories, but this tactic *works.*

Make it pleasant for yourself to do what you want to be doing—better yet, make it downright pleasurable. We've been doing this in your experiments and exercises, having you get good feelings every time you do what you want to be doing. We're making these good feelings your automatic habit.

At first you might have to pause and allow yourself to feel them after doing something for yourself. After a while it will become spontaneous. The principle is: *Always, always, always give yourself an immediate, pleasurable payoff, and you'll both enjoy taking care of yourself and find that your new, desired conduct quickly becomes your self-reinforcing, spontaneous habit.*

Exercise Seven: Practicing Self-Hypnosis
Purpose
    To obtain the benefits of self-hypnosis.
Method
    Self-hypnosis, as instructed above.

Directions

Duplicate the following page from the book and use it to guide yourself in doing the session. Write your formula in the place indicated. Do 5 to 10 brief sessions daily your first week—just go through the exercise very quickly, taking one to three minutes each time. Thereafter, practice two or three times daily, each session 5 to 30 minutes long.

Basic Self-Hypnosis Routine

1. TOUCH a finger to the center of your forehead, close your eyes and STARE at that spot, return your hand to your side or your lap.

2. TAKE A DEEP BREATH and TENSE all your muscles at once, or just the muscles of your butt and bottom.

3. BREATHE OUT when you cannot hold your breath any longer with comfort, exhaling as slowly as you can while you RELAX your muscles, and let your eyes ROLL DOWN as slowly as you can.

4. WHISPER "ZERO" to yourself with the last of your breath as you exhale, and LET YOURSELF GO COMPLETELY LIMP.

5. REPEAT "ZERO" over and over to yourself. You may combine this with squeezing and relaxing your eyes.

6. SAY YOUR FORMULA to yourself when you are ready. Write it out here:

_____

_____

_____

_____

_____

7. REPEAT your formula to yourself and imagine it as you do so.

8. VISUALIZE your formula, using all the senses and symbols you can. Let your mind drift, imagine it coming true or remember the future. When done, let the image shrink into a dot and vanish.

9. (Here use any other self-hypnosis techniques you'd like.)

10. END YOUR SESSION, when ready, by repeating your formula to yourself, taking a deep breath, and counting up from 1 to 10. Open your eyes and feel all the exhilarating and beneficial effects. You'll feel calm, peaceful, wide awake, simply wonderful.

EIGHT

Strategies for Solving Problems

Your basic self-hypnosis routine is itself an effective way for attaining better self-management, for relieving stress and tension, or for programming yourself for long-term success. As a self-management strategy, it works indirectly in that these benefits will gradually develop as you continue your daily practice of the exercise. Some will occur sooner than others; the more earnestly you practice, the more likely a quicker result.

However, once you feel comfortable with your basic exercise, you can learn to use more specifically focused hypnotic tactics for dealing with your more immediate problems and situations. You begin working with them in part nine of your basic exercise, but may then go on to use many problem-solving strategies on an informal, on-the-spot basis outside of your actual sessions.

For our purposes, we can define a problem as *a situation in which you find yourself blocked in some way.* Therefore, it hangs up in time, persisting as an unresolved threat to your success or survival. In order to rid yourself of the problem, you need to figure out the situation and find some way to change it.

The key to resolving problems is always change. By

bringing about an appropriate change in the situation, you can resolve whatever has become a problem to you.

To most easily and effectually do this, you should begin by making an assessment of the situation. Use your self-assessment technique (Key Technique One), focusing your questions appropriately. For example, ask yourself, "What's bugging me about my behavior under pressure?" It's best to write out your answers.

What you can do about it depends on the situation. Sometimes you can find a way to take immediate, direct action to help resolve it. Often, your problem relates to your long-term self-management goals—but even then, you'll want to do something to rid yourself of it. Frequently, you will use your basic self-hypnosis routine to relieve stress, motivate yourself, etc. However, you will generally wish to employ some combination of four basic strategies to introduce the necessary change in yourself or your situation to resolve your problems.

Redefining the Situation

As you probably recall, the definition-of-the-situation concept states that whatever you accept to be real will be real in its consequences for you. You can turn this simple premise to great advantage in problem-solving work. The strategy is to *define or redefine the situation to bring about changes helping resolve whatever about it is a problem for you.*

One of the most elegant ways of employing this strategy is to create tactics that will work for you because you've programmed yourself to believe they will work. Accept the idea that they will have thus and such an effect, and they will; it's a matter of your meanings, not of objective reality.

We are familiar with this in everyday life. For example, do you like a good steak? Does the thought of a fancy steak dinner make your mouth water? How do you feel when you treat yourself to something like this?

Why, then, would the same idea make a good Hindu nauseous? It can't be something about steak itself—rather, it's a matter of the definitions of the situation, conditioned into you from childhood. And we're not talking about matters of opinion: The Hindu would actually feel nausea; your mouth might actually water. These are spontaneous, gut-level responses based on your deeply engrained beliefs and understandings.

Using your self-hypnosis, you can create new gut-level meanings for yourself that can have similar effect. One way of employing this principle is to *define objects, events, or actions in a new way, or to identify new "realities" for yourself.*

A dramatic example is the case of a nervous gentleman who came to me for relief from unbearable stress, tension, and anxiety. He had nursed his elderly father through a heart attack, only to have the man die of another coronary after a prolonged convalescence. Now middle-aged himself, my client lived in fear of dying of a heart attack. I noticed that unconsciously, as he spoke, the man would touch a trembling hand to his own chest, as if to reassure himself that his heart was okay. He did this continuously, a kind of nervous habit.

What I did was quite standard. First, I taught him progressive relaxation. In the next session I introduced him to a hypnosis session similar to those you've worked with. In the third week I taught him self-hypnosis. The only new thing I added was a suggestion that whenever he felt uptight or nervous, he could immediately calm himself by touching one hand to his heart.

Bingo! That resolved his case.

Using hypnosis, I helped him define a new meaning to his long-standing habit. We thus created a situation in which the more he indulged in conduct he has come to associate with feeling distressed, the more he would soothe and calm himself. Obviously, there was no causal relationship between what he did and his response to doing that.

There didn't have to be any—it's all done with meanings.

This example clearly illustrates the sort of things you can accomplish through redefinition. It also exemplifies three specific problem-solving tactics by which you can make use of this general strategy.

The first is that *by using your thinking and imagining, you can create whatever connections you desire by defining such a relationship to exist.* Everything else flows from this.

Secondly, we not only created a new connection between what he was doing and what he was feeling, but we turned his meanings upside down. When confronted with a "stuck" pattern of behavior or response keeping you locked into a problem, *you can redefine a behavior or kind of event to mean or cause something other than what it has always implied for you.* Overeaters, smokers, and substance abusers can, for example, redefine the object of their cravings to be something they can now take or leave. This simple ploy aligns their imagination and their will so that their mind begins to work for rather than against them.

However, I didn't select just any cue, but this gentleman's automatic habit of touching his heart. This involves one of the oldest tricks in the book: *Make what you would do anyway or what would happen regardless serve your own purposes.* Use this approach to add real clout to other tactics. It is particularly useful for turning around compulsive behaviors and responses.

One way of doing this is to deliberately create a new habit for yourself, either a habit of mind or of actual conduct. In your homework for nervous habits (Key Technique Two), for example, you defined any urge for a cigarette or other object of craving to remind you to take a sip of water. Not only is water good for you, it satisfies your mouth's craving; and taking a sip of water will require you to take your attention off the temptation while you get the drink. Nine times out of ten, this will eliminate any sense of having to give in to the nervous habit, leaving you with a con-structive, healthful habit in its place.

A related device is to use some other cue than "zero" in your basic self-hypnosis routine. Your choice should directly relate to your goals. Select a one- or two-syllable word that feels right to you. A golfing client of mine, for example, did extremely well substituting the word "birdie."

The simplest tactic, however, is direct suggestion. While somewhat limited in its application, this technique can be used in part nine of your routine, or even outside hypnosis. Simply tell yourself what you need to hear, in the best way you can state it. Use all the tricks you are learning, including the fact that you are generally much more able to accept suggestions when deeply relaxed and in a hypnotic frame of mind.

In problem solving, suggestions are used to define and prompt. Just as with your self-hypnosis formula, *to get the most out of suggestions, you should imagine along with what you are telling yourself.* A fantasy is usually best, but you can simply imagine hearing or reading what you are saying. You could picture the words printed, typewritten, or in your handwriting. They can be in a book or on a screen, ticker tape, or telegram. They might be coming out of a tele-vision or radio, or written in fire in the sky. Anything you can imagine is okay.

Key Technique Six: Direct Suggestion (Getting to Sleep)
Use

Changing the situation by defining or promoting thoughts, feelings, or actions, as appropriate. To illustrate, we will use the example of a sleep suggestion given within self-hypnosis to overcome insomnia or allow you to get back to sleep if you awaken in the middle of the night.

Method

In part nine of your basic routine, or at some other time when you can be receptive, tell yourself a suggestion and imagine or drift along as appropriate. Then go on to your next thing to do in the session or elsewhere.

Example

Say to yourself, "As soon as I count to ten, I can just close my eyes again and drift into a deep, natural, refreshing sleep lasting until [time you wish to wake up]." Imagine along as you say it. Complete your basic exercise, then close your eyes and let your mind drift— even if you never fall into a regular sleep, several hours of this deeply relaxed state will be just as healthful and refreshing, so don't worry, just let yourself drift off.

Variation

For sleep only, merely *imagine* going through part ten of your routine. Imagine ending your session and then let yourself drift off.

Another technique especially valuable in redefining the situation is a simple form of visualization in which you imagine that the reality is already as you want it to be. *You lead with make-believe, and the actuality will follow if you let it.* Just imagine yourself thinking, feeling, acting, and responding as you wish. We might call this the technique of *as-if imagining.*

As-if imagining is the basic stratagem I use in my hypnosis sessions with others. Therefore, you will see it as the predominant tactic in your session scripts. For example, I've asked you to imagine floating like a caterpillar in the cocoon, and feeling as if you were already feeling the good feelings you'll always get from doing hypnosis or self-hypnosis.

Note also that I consistently use lots of sensory language and imagery. In normal speech, you wouldn't use so many "feels" in a single sentence. However, in hypnosis, it makes good sense to "feel as if you were already feeling the good feelings." That takes it out of the realm of thinking-about and into the realm of allowing-yourself-to-experience.

Whenever possible, convert your ideas into something you can feel or experience, and imagine that.

By using this technique of as-if imagining, you are triggering your normal learning processes, but you are allowing yourself to learn from imaginary rather than objective experience. You build an imaginary occurrence illustrating a desired reality or a changed reality, you allow yourself to experience this in make-believe, and you find yourself spontaneously tending to act as if it already were as you've defined it to be. The make-believe always comes first, the reality follows.

Key Technique Seven: As-If Imagining.
Use

To create new realities for yourself through make-believe.

Method

Visualization.

Directions

Imagine a scene, experience, or episode as if the reality already was as you'd want it to be. Allow yourself to fully perceive and respond to this fantasy in your imagination, as if it already were true. Do this in part nine of your self-hypnosis routine, in progressive relaxation, or otherwise as appropriate.

Creating Desired Responses

Another strategy is more direct yet. You *use visualization to elicit or create desired responses.* On the spot, this approach can be used to evoke any psychosomatic responses you'd like, from relieving pain to deliberately stimulating adrenalinelike responses to increase your level of alertness or physical energy. You can use a similar method in your routine self-hypnosis as a rehearsal technique, to shape your natural response when on the spot later.

The technique you use for these purposes has been

described by N. P. Spanos as *goal-directed imagining*. He found that people who did well on tests of hypnosis were all doing something alike; they were imagining situations that would, in actuality, bring about the response being suggested. If they were being given a suggestion that they couldn't open their eyes, for example, they might—all by themselves—imagine that their eyes were being glued shut. Those who didn't actively involve themselves by some cognitive strategy of this sort generally did much less well at experiencing classic hypnotic responses than those who did.

We've used Spanos's principle throughout this volume. Specifically, however, goal-directed imagining refers to visualizations in which you deliberately imagine something that would cause or explain the effect you desire to experience. You've done this in, for example, the visualizations of Exercise Three. Now you can use the same tactic as a problem-solving strategy.

Key Technique Eight: Using Goal-Directed Imagining
Use

To bring about desired responses, feelings, and psychosomatic behaviors at will.

Method

Visualization, in part nine of the basic routine, as an informal technique outside of hypnosis, or after any relaxation or induction technique as appropriate. The identical principle is employed in many other techniques you are using.

Directions

Deliberately imagine a situation, scene, or episode that would cause, involve, or otherwise trigger the feelings, behaviors, or other responses you desire. This will work almost immediately, on the spot. Practiced in your routine self-hypnosis, it can, in effect, condition you to allow yourself to respond the same way afterward, in real-life situations.

Example

Rather than direct suggestion, you could use goal-directed imagining for insomnia. Visualize a situation in which you couldn't help but fall asleep, one in which you simply couldn't keep awake. Some people might like to imagine falling into a pleasant stupor from drink, drugs, or after sex; others might prefer to remember a time they were so exhausted after productive and satisfying physical exertion that they fell asleep the moment they lay down. You might also consider a fantasy of a magical or fairy-tale kind. Whatever you choose to imagine, really build it up with lots and lots of sensory cues, and allow yourself to respond. You might like to *first* imagine ending your session, *then* do this visualization, rather than the other way around.

These last three techniques form the basis of most others you will be working with. Before you try them out, however, let me introduce you to a tactic we will use in your experiments and which you could conceivably use in your own self-hypnosis.

Key Technique Nine: Cue Cards
(Arons Prehypnotic Suggestion Method)

Use

In training, as an alternative to prepared scripts. In routine practice, to replace or supplement formal suggestions, to help organizing visualizations, or as an aid when learning new suggestions. Harry Arons, a leading professional hypnotist, developed this technique to replace entirely suggestions within self-hypnosis.

Method

Prepare an index card or sheet of paper on which you write out your suggestion, session goal, or themes for visualization. Immediately before starting your self-hypnosis procedure, read over your card a few times. Let the suggestions run through your mind as you do the self-hypnosis. You can also use your cards within the actual session: Open your eyes, read over the card, close your eyes, say a few zeros, and continue.

Experiment Sixteen: Three Basic Problem-Solving Techniques

Purpose

To familiarize yourself with the three basic problem-solving techniques.

Method

Self-hypnosis with cue cards.

Directions

Prepare three cards as follows. On one card, print the numeral *1*, and beneath this, the words *direct suggestion*. Underneath that, write your theme, *I'm having fun doing self-hypnosis*. On your second card, write *2*, below that write *as-if imagining*, and beneath that your theme, *I'm having more fun doing self-hypnosis with every new beat of my heart*. On the last card, write *3*, *goal-directed imagining*, and the theme, *I'm feeling an intense sensation of pleasure*. Stack the cards with number one on top, number three on the bottom.

To actually do the experiment, do your basic self-hypnosis routine to part five, where you'd normally say your formula. Instead, this time, open your eyes, read over your first card several times, close your eyes, say "zero" a few times, and then give yourself the suggestion on your card. Imagine reading the suggestion as you give it to yourself. Then end your session as usual.

Open your eyes and place the first card to one side so that card number two is on top of the deck. Read the card over a few times and then do your self-hypnosis, again to the point where you'd normally say your formula. This time, with or without opening your eyes to read the card again—don't bother to do so if you remember the theme—imagine that you are indeed having more and more fun doing self-hypnosis with every beat of your heart. When you are ready, end your session and again open your eyes.

This time, put the second card off to one side and read over your third card several times. Again do your self-hypnosis induction to the point where you'd normally give yourself the formula. This time, visualize a real or imaginary situation in which you would, indeed, feel an intense sensation of pleasure. Really build it up, using symbols and sensory detail. When ready, end your session and open your eyes. *As you open your eyes, tell yourself that you will clearly remember everything you felt, did, or experienced during this experiment.* Make whatever notes you feel appropriate in your journal regarding how it went and ideas for effectively using these three strategies on your own.

Eliminating Undesired Responses

Another strategy, especially useful as an informal tactic when on the spot, is to eliminate or let go of undesired responses. This begins very much like redefining meanings, in that you create for yourself a cue to which you can tie the act of relaxing and letting go of the response, feeling, or tension you don't wish to indulge in at the time. You have been working with one of these techniques from your first introduction to strategic hypnosis.

Key Technique Ten: The Zero Technique *(Pausing Before You Act)*
Use

To clear your mind, calm yourself, and maximize your ability to meet the demands of any situation.

Method

An informal self-hypnosis tactic.

Directions

> Before you act or respond, or when anything requires your attention or effort, or simply to clear your mind and calm yourself at any time, take a deeper than usual breath and say, picture, and/or feel zero to yourself. Now breathe out and go on to whatever you were about to do. While most effective with your eyes closed and taking a very deep breath, it will work well enough for most purposes with your eyes open and only a slightly deeper than usual breath; nobody has to know you are using this tactic.

I teach two additional techniques of this sort to practically all my students and clients, usually in their first session. All three work on the principle of training yourself to use them in self-hypnosis, then using them as informal techniques on the spot.

Key Technique Eleven: The Stop Technique (Changing Mental Tracks)
Use

> At any time, in any situation, to change your thinking from negative and unwanted to positive and desired.

Method

> An informal self-hypnosis tactic.

Directions

> With your eyes open or closed, yell the word *stop* to yourself with all your might, while visualizing a stop sign or stoplight. When around others or in public, do this inside your head; if alone you can actually yell the word *stop* as loud as you'd like. It's best in either case to combine this with all the physical motions of straining to yell at the top of your lungs. This tactic works partly because you define it to work and partly because you simply can't do all this and keep on thinking or acting at the same time. It breaks the flow and

enables you to snap into a desirable mental track immediately.

Key Technique Twelve: Letting Go of Unwanted Feelings

Use

At any time, in any situation, to let go of inappropriate or unwanted feelings and similar responses without having to fight them or suffer.

Method

An informal self-hypnosis tactic.

Directions

Proceed as in the zero technique—take a deep breath, close your eyes, and say "zero" to yourself. Then, as you exhale forcefully, imagine and say to yourself a suggestion like, "I don't have to feel this way—I'm free!" Let yourself imagine breathing this feeling out by its very roots as you do this. If the feelings seem especially hard to expel, blow out hard a few more times while repeating your suggestion and imagining that you are, indeed, blowing these feelings out and away. You might prefer another suggestion than the above; many clients like "I'm free," while others use something unprintable.

These three simple techniques illustrate how you can train yourself in self-hypnosis to work with informal, on-the-spot tactics. As a rule, *do not wait until you are confronted with an actual problem, but rather, prepare yourself to cope with problems when you are not on the spot, but relaxed and practicing your routine self-hypnosis.* Hundreds of my clients and students have found these three techniques for eliminating undesired responses to be particularly helpful in dealing with problem situations and learning better self-management.

There is a practical rationale behind such tactics. This was described by early students of general semantics as the "corticothalamic pause." The basic idea is to break the flow of your thinking, feeling, and responding to the situation as you define it to be, so that you can pay attention to the actual situation as it happens to be in present time and act appropriately; in other words, to help you stop blocking yourself by responding to your own imaginations concerning the situation.

Experiment Seventeen: Letting Go of Undesired Responses

Purpose

    To begin training yourself in the above three informal techniques for letting go of undesired responses.

Method

    Self-hypnosis with cue cards.

Directions

    Make up two cue cards. On the first, write *One,* and the words *changing mental tracks.* Beneath this, on separate lines, write *1. Remember/imagine a time I was really bothered by negative, self-defeating thoughts, 2. Really build it up,* and *3. Now picture a stop sign or stoplight while yelling STOP to myself.* On your second card, write *Two,* the words *letting go of unwanted feelings,* and, on separate lines below this, write *1. Remember/imagine a time I was really bothered by bad feelings of stress, guilt, anxiety, self-consciousness, or panic, 2. Really build them up,* and *3. Now take a deep breath, say zero, say* I don't have to feel this way—I'm free! *and blow all the bad feelings out of my mind and body.* Stack the cards in order.

    You will proceed exactly as in your last experiment. Read over the first card, do your self-hypnosis to the point where you normally say your formula; open your eyes; read the card over again; close your eyes; and do steps 1, 2, and 3; complete your session; and open your eyes. Now read the second card and do the same thing. The secret will be to really build up the problem situation in your imagination, allowing your mind and body to actually respond as they have in the past when this sort of thing has happened to you, and then to use the technique as if it could not help but do the trick for you. You might want to keep on practicing these two tactics in part nine of your routine self-hypnosis, with or without the cards, until you can comfortably use these tactics when actually on the spot. There is no need to separately practice the zero technique; just use it whenever appropriate. You want to make this pause a matter of habit.

Unblocking Performance by Imaginative Rehearsal

The fourth major problem-solving technique is based upon what you have learned with regard to the others. In effect, it combines elements of all of them in a new way. The strategy is to rehearse your desired performances or other conduct in make-believe until you are able to do the same thing in the real world.

This strategy works with the fact that we are all the time running simulations of reality through our mental "computer." We continually fit what we are experiencing into our total sense of what is really going on in the outside world. One of the liabilities of this process is that we react more or less subconsciously to our own thinking and imagining about that external reality, just as we do to actual perceptions.

These subtle reactions to ourselves become part of the picture we don't think we are putting there—and that becomes a problem. We tend, for example, to rationalize our nonrational responses by making our ideas about reality conform to our feelings, whether or not they are actually appropriate to what we are experiencing.

More than this, as we react to our own thinking and even to the words with which we think to ourselves, we tend to become increasingly divorced from what we can actually perceive of the external situation. For example, we tend to dwell upon negative scenarios in which we imagine the worst possible interpretation or consequences to the situations confronting us.

Like the flight-or-fight response, this is probably a primitive tactic for keeping ourselves out of danger. We tend to feel anxious about and avoid situations that seem likely to turn out badly for us. Scenarios that generate strong negative feelings of this sort tend to stick in our minds, perhaps because these feelings make them seem so real to us.

However, this response tends to entrap us. Each time we imagine something in negative terms of threat and failure, we evoke feelings and total body responses associated with danger and possible loss. Before we know it, we are liable to have talked ourselves into accepting this negative definition of the situation as inevitable, natural, how it "really" must be. Then, if we can't entirely avoid the situation, we tend to act out these negative ideas and so cause ourselves to blow it.

By this process, you make yourself uptight, anxious, tense. You block yourself from applying your true potentialities for making the situation go right for you. Rather than giving it all you've got, you tend to turn your worst fears and imaginings into self-fulfilling prophecies.

This kind of blockage is known as *performance anxiety.* This term was first used in the field of sexuality counseling to describe the general situation where you are so worried about how you will do that your attention becomes stuck on the details of trying to give an adequate performance, you make yourself tense or even panicky, and so you block yourself from being able to do what you could have done if only you had *relaxed* and *allowed yourself* to do it.

Fortunately, you can use self-hypnotic techniques to turn this situation around and even positively facilitate your performance. This problem-solving strategy has you *use the linkages between thinking, feeling, imagining, and overall performance to both dispel performance anxiety and also to create self-fulfilling prophecies of a positive nature.* By imaginative rehearsal you dispel fears, anxieties, and negative imaginings while creating a positive mental attitude and definition of the situation.

One way of doing this is to first imagine the worst possible outcome, letting yourself experience all the bad feelings and negative consequences that would result from your totally blowing it. Then you imagine the opposite, making everything work out perfectly. By practicing this kind of visualization, you make it clear to yourself that there is nothing to fear, that the very worst that could happen is not nearly so bad as you've feared—and that you really can allow yourself to make it work out right for you and to perform at your maximum potential.

Unlike the other problem-solving strategies, this one is never used as an informal tactic when on the spot. Rather, it is a training device you must use in part nine of your basic self-hypnosis to shape your mental habits. For it to really benefit you, you must practice working on a situation or kind of situation over days or weeks. Therefore, you will want to begin working with this technique long before you will be faced with the actual situation. Of course, if you have no choice in the matter, you can work with imaginative rehearsals at any time.

Key Technique Thirteen: Imaginative Rehearsals
Use

> To relieve performance anxiety and any other blockages, and to positively set yourself up for maximum performance in any tests, challenges, difficult interpersonal or social situations, performances of any kind, or other problems and situations you might be worried about or particularly need or want to bring off well.

Method

> Guided visualization, always done in part nine of your basic self-hypnosis or its equivalent. Note: For best results, you should begin practicing imaginative rehearsals

as long as possible before the actual time when you must deal with the problem. The more you practice, the better prepared you will be.

Directions

There are essentially three parts to the exercise.

1. Bring to mind the situation or performance you will work on. Now imagine the day arrives when you must actually deal with it. Imagine everything going wrong for you—getting up late in the morning in a foul mood, perhaps with a cold or a hangover, everything going wrong throughout the day up till the actual time of the performance, and then imagine that everything that could go wrong does. Just envision your worst fears coming true as you really blow it—put in all the negative details such as your hands trembling, your armpits dripping, your mind going blank, as well as everything else you've feared about making a fool of yourself.

2. Now let the negative feelings really build up. Imagine everyone around you reacting to your failure—everything you would yourself feel or experience were you to blow it in this terrible fashion. Collapse all the negative fears and feelings upon yourself and further build up this sense of ultimate disaster by slowly counting "one, two, three," and imagining the bad feelings growing stronger and more real to you with each count. By "three" they should feel excruciating, almost unbearably bad for you, totally real. Then, after "three," take a deep breath, say "zero" to yourself and blow all the air out of your lungs forcefully while saying or thinking "I refuse to feel this way!" Keep on blowing out with all your might until all the bad feelings are gone, as if they are completely rinsed out of your system, leaving you calm, light-headed, and relaxed. It shouldn't take more than five or six times blowing out to rid yourself of even the worst feelings.

3. Next, you want to imagine everything going perfectly for you, yourself making everything go right. Imagine, perhaps, waking up the morning of the problem situation after a refreshing night's sleep, doing self-hypnosis before getting out of bed, visualizing everything working out right, then getting up and smoothly moving through your day. Imagine that immediately before you must actually deal with the test or problem you do self-hypnosis again, and then visualize yourself using everything you know to make the situation go right for you. Imagine everything working out exactly as you would realistically hope to make it work out. Then let yourself feel the reactions of yourself and others to your tremendous success, really allowing yourself to build up and experience all these good feelings of pride, accomplishment, mastery, etc. Enjoy the good feelings for as long as you'd like, then complete your session.

Variation

Immediately before the test or performance, you will neither need nor want to visualize the negative scenario in steps 1 and 2. Just do step 3 as a "positive rehearsal." Also use this positive rehearsal approach if you merely want to psych yourself up and boost performance; if you have no strong concerns, worries, or anxieties about the situation to begin with; or—contrarily—if you are simply *too* tense, fearful, and uptight about it to feel comfortable about visualizing the worst possible scenario.

Imaginative rehearsal is one of your most powerful and most generally applicable strategies. It is particularly useful in social, sexual, professional, and other "performing" situations to overcome stage fright, fears, guilts, or any other anxiety regarding your performance—including rejection, shyness, lack of assertiveness, or fear of success or of accepting pleasure and gratification. Clients have very successfully used this method to help improve performance in sales, public speaking, sports, and examinations, in the performing arts, or just to handle family hassles, office politics, or other "business as usual."

Other Problem-Solving Tactics

There is no limit on the possible tactics you can develop for use in strategic self-hypnosis. Any book on hypnosis, self-hypnosis, popular psychology, or self-help will suggest a host of additional ways of overcoming problems.

In particular, the methods of behavior therapy and cognitive-behavioral counseling can be adapted for use in strategic self-hypnosis. These will usually involve relaxation followed by visualization or suggestion. Other tactics may be done entirely outside hypnosis. Several approaches of this sort have been mentioned with regard to nervous habits, while others will be suggested later in this book.

You might, for example, want to work on mild phobic reactions such as specific fears regarding flying, heights, bugs, and snakes. You could, in such a case, work with some of the techniques of desensitization that you can find in books on the subject. These fit right into your self-hypnosis routine. Alternatively, you might simply work with such fears in the imaginative rehearsal technique just described. Play it safe, however, by first seeking professional assistance with any really heavy or crippling fears, problems, or difficulties.

The basic techniques of imaginative rehearsal, direct suggestion, and as-if imagining are especially adaptable to dealing with specific problems and situations. Goal-directed imagining is normally done as a part of these other techniques. However, there may be times when you want a nondirective way for working on your problems—specifically, when you have not been able to come up with an effective or practical way to go about resolving them. Here's a technique that will facilitate your creative problem-solving potential:

Key Technique Fourteen: Drifting

Use

Either as a way of imagining suggestions (as in Chapter Seven) or as a problem-solving tactic. You can also use drifting as a meditation technique, or to unblock your creativity in writing, the arts, etc.

Method

Nondirective visualization or imagining. Normally done within self-hypnosis.

Directions

If you are working on a specific problem area or within a particular theme, you might want to first prepare a cue card stating that theme or problem. You can either read the card before self-hypnosis or immediately before working with this technique. This step is optional.

In part nine of the basic exercise, say a few zeros to further relax yourself, and then just let your mind wander along the theme (as in drifting along with your suggestion, in Chapter Seven), or just let yourself imagine along with whatever comes into your mind. You might first go over in your mind what you hope to accomplish, then say the zeros and see what your mind comes up with. Let yourself fantasize, imagining possible solutions, no matter how sketchy, silly, or unreal. In effect, let yourself meditate on the problem or theme; as many counselors say, let your unconscious play with the problem.

Suggestion: It is wise to have a pencil and paper by your side while using this technique. As you think of new ideas, insights, or approaches, just open your eyes and jot them down. Then close your eyes, say a few zeros and continue. If you find your creativity really flowing, it is perfectly okay to forget about your session and just set to work.

Alternatively, you can remain in session and let your mind wander as it will until you're ready to end your self-hypnosis. Before you do so, tell yourself that you'll be able to remember all the ideas you've thought of and that you will find your creativity or problem solving fully unblocked. Then count up, open your eyes, jot down your notes, and continue.

Variation

As a meditation technique or to generally free up your creativity, use drifting in place of the suggestion and visualization portions of the standard routine.

Programming Yourself

Self-hypnosis is really a training device. Its purpose is to help you learn how to tap your full potential. Closing our consideration of problem-solving strategies is a method that clearly illustrates this point. In *setting your mind*, you don't need to go through any rigamarole. You just do it; you program your desired course of action. It never hurts to first go through your zero technique, but that is not really necessary. Once you have learned to guide yourself with self-hypnosis, you can just go ahead and define the situation you wish to create or experience in your imagination and then allow yourself to act out this script.

Key Technique Fifteen: Setting Your Mind

Use

Any time—to enhance performance, steer or shape your conduct in a certain way, etc.

Method

An informal technique used on the spot.

Directions

If you'd like, you can combine this with the zero technique, starting by taking a deep breath and saying "zero" to yourself. However, this is optional.

Otherwise, start by closing your eyes and inhaling deeply. After this or after saying "zero," tell yourself or think to yourself what you want to do, how you intend to make the situation work out. Do this in concrete, even sensory detail. Then briefly visualize yourself following this script. Open your eyes and just do it—keeping an "allowing," calm, and positive attitude as you proceed to act. The whole process should take no more than a couple of seconds.

Example

I am learning downhill skiing. Before I take off down the slope, I close my eyes, say "zero," and tell myself how I wish to do it—that I will stay relaxed and balanced, keeping my weight on the downhill ski, maneuvering in such and such a fashion. Then I briefly visualize myself skiing this way, with grace and good technique. I open my eyes and slide downhill, keeping myself relaxed and poised to do my very best yet.

Experiment Eighteen: Using Imaginative Problem-Solving Techniques

Purpose

To gain experience with drifting, imaginative rehearsal, and mind-setting techniques.

Method

Self-hypnosis with cue card.

Directions

Prepare one cue card. Think of a situation, test, challenge, or performance coming up in the near future about which you are at all nervous, self-conscious, or worried. On your cue card, write down what this is. Then, below that, write 1. *Imagine blowing it*, under which write 2. *Build up, 1-2-3, Blow out*, beneath which write 3. *Imagine making it go right*. Use these to remind yourself how to do the imaginative rehearsal (review Key Technique Thirteen if you'd like).

Give yourself a session as follows. First, set your mind. Tell yourself you are going to have a wonderful session in which you will do an imaginary rehearsal and really get something out of it, and then you will let your mind drift along some interesting or pleasurable theme. Then briefly visualize how that might be.

Now go through your routine self-hypnosis exercise all the way to part nine. At this point, if you'd like, you can open your eyes and read the cue card. If you remember what you've planned to do, leave your eyes closed. Now go through the three steps of the imaginative rehearsal technique.

Then say a few zeros, perhaps even squeezing and relaxing your eyes as you do so. Once you feel really comfortable and dreamy again, just let your mind wander and drift along whatever interesting and pleasant themes it comes up with. (Variation: If there is a really important problem situation, or something you are really confused and uncertain about, you could think about that here. Begin by thinking about—but then let your mind begin to drift along—that theme.) When you are ready, complete your session and make some notes in your journal about how it went, how these techniques felt to you, any interesting observations or ideas—or, for that matter, anything you figured out during this session regarding your problems.

NINE

Psychosomatic Self-Control

Psychosomatic refers to the fact that what goes on in your mind influences what happens in your body, and vice versa. Not only can you use self-hypnosis to help you do things better in the external world, but you can also apply the strategic approach to reach within yourself and take charge over bodily functions and responses.

Actually, the power to do so is your inborn potential. The art of psychosomatic self-control is a skill which, like all other skills, must be developed through training and practice. In this chapter we will not talk about psychosomatic strategies so much as strategies for developing your self-control skills.

Your entire physical organism is already moving in a perpetual dance to your feeling and thinking. Yet mental acts are also acts of your body. They are not something occurring within some metaphysical organ called your brain, but something you do with your brain and the rest of your organism. There is now conclusive laboratory evidence that you can learn a surprising degree of control over even the so-called involuntary functions of the body by directing your thinking and imagining strategically.

Autonomic control of this kind was long imagined to

be impossible by Western science. It simply did not fit the way educated people looked at the world. Their modern world view was based on the idea of *dualism*—the concept that mind and body are distinct, separate things.

Those who believed it was possible to influence things by thinking were relegated to the lunatic or occultist fringe. Even hypnosis was treated this way until recently. After all, even supporters could only explain these things as "mind over matter," and that was manifestly ridiculous.

"Mind over matter" is, indeed, the wrong idea. However, the equally wrong ideas of mechanical science blocked progress in this area until the 1960s. Then, legitimate scientists began to investigate the seemingly impossible feats of Hindu yogis and other practitioners of self-control disciplines. What they found has revolutionized medical and behavioral science.

It is not "mind over matter" at all. It's much, much simpler and more marvelous than that. What we call your mind is something you do with and through your physical organism; you are a psychosomatic whole. Mind is a process by which we become conscious of ourselves and by which we humans manage ourselves, as described in Chapter Two.

Science has been forced to concede that there is no actual separation between mind and body. Both are aspects of being human. Your body is the biological hardware supporting your existence in this world. Your mind is what you do with that hunk of protoplasm. Our uniquely human mental processes are our species' most important tool for survival, the means by which we have gained preeminence over all the earth.

Thinking that you have a mind located somehow in your head or brain controlling your body as a master controls the slave only blocks you from realizing your true potentialities. It is a false belief. Your mind is a function of your entire organism. Body and mind are ways of looking at the same thing.

By consciously directing your thinking, feeling, and imagining, you can extend voluntary control even to those bodily processes that are normally involuntary and self-regulating. In this chapter we will consider the ways in which you can use this fact to your best advantage.

Mind-Body Linkages

What you will be doing is to exploit the countless ways in which mind and body are linked together. In psychosomatic self-control, you will use your mental acts to indirectly shape your physical responses. You must do this indirectly; you simply cannot do it directly, by acts of will.

The idea that you can control psychosomatic response through acts of the will is implied by the phrase "mind over matter." While scientists dismissed the possibility out of hand, others believed that this was the way in which yogis performed their stunts and in which hypnotic responses were brought about.

That proved to be incorrect. You *can* learn to do almost any of the things you have heard that Indian fakirs and yogis can do, or that subjects who have been hypnotized can do. But you'll never accomplish these things by willpower.

Mind-body linkages just do not work that way. Nor do you have to use any psychic abilities for this purpose. It's much simpler than you ever expected.

Your mind and body functions are interconnected. Using the one to control the other does not require psychic abilities but rather, making use of existing, objective psychosomatic linkages. The key to this whole area of your inborn human potentialities is—you guessed it, I'm sure—your imagination. Once again, the power you need is your old familiar imagination power.

What happens when you apply your imagination strategically to control bodily processes is not mysterious or magical in the least. As you have learned from the experiments in this book, your body responds to your thinking, feeling, and imagining with the same kinds of responses with which it reacts to "real" events. Your body is a sort of robot of limited discernment and intelligence; it depends on your mind for judgment and direction. Visualize yourself in danger, about to be torn apart by wild animals, and your body reacts with a flight-or-fight response.

Experiment Nineteen: Psychosomatic Responses
Purpose

To explore ways of voluntarily controlling physical functions.

Method

Read and do, no need to tape or use formal self-hypnosis.

Directions

There are two parts to this experiment. First, close your eyes and try to make yourself salivate. Use willpower to make your mouth water. After a minute or so, open your eyes and record your results.

For the second part, close your eyes again. This time, use goal-directed imagining (Key Technique Eight). Using all senses, remember or make up a fantasy experience in which you were simply ravenous and could see, smell, and taste anything and everything that would be mouth-watering for you. Really build up this visualization of taste buds' heaven. After a minute or two, let the imagination go away and open your eyes.

Jot down some notes about the differential effects of using willpower and imagining. What happened in each case? What does part two tell you about the things you crave? Do you respond to the things themselves, to acts of will, or to your imaginations?

Salivation is normally an involuntary process. Pavlov showed that you can condition dogs to salivate by association. We go one step further: *You can use your imagination to indirectly get at and control bodily processes you simply cannot influence directly.*

You can learn to do some amazing things in this fashion. There is, for example, conclusive evidence that at least some women can increase their busts through self-hypnotic means. Less spectacularly, most of us can learn to change the temperature of various parts of our bodies, to relieve pain and discomfort, perhaps to facilitate healing processes. You have already become skillful at one psychosomatic task, alleviating muscular tension.

Engineering considerations alone limit what you can do; there must always be a biological potentiality to work with. Many psychosomatic abilities involve conscious control over blood circulation. Exactly how this works is being clarified at the present time. Other mechanisms, such as that behind breast enlargement, are not yet understood. However, there is no question that this too will prove to involve some built-in capability of the human organism.

Biofeedback

I am often asked how all this relates to biofeedback. I explain that this term technically describes using meters and other instruments to tell you what is happening in your body. The neat thing about these devices is that they respond instantly to changes in skin temperature, electrical resistance, muscle tension, or some other indicator of your body's state, letting you know if what you are doing has the desired effect as you are doing it. This can be very helpful in mastering psychosomatic self-control skills.

For a small percentage of cases, this mechanical feedback is the only way to learn these skills. However, being hooked up to biofeedback apparatus does not significantly change what you have to do. You will still work in the same way. If you have access to quality biofeedback equipment, by all means learn how to use it; this equipment can make it quite a bit easier to master the art of psychosomatic self-control. It's not, though, anything you can't do as well without.

The most widely popularized form of biofeedback, brain waves, is no longer much used by scientists and clinicians. It proved far less than it was cracked up to be. Still, one pattern of your brain's electrical activity, called *alpha waves,* is touted as the key to hypnosis and psychosomatic control. Don't concern yourself with brain waves; there are much more useful and more accurate indicators of your internal state.

Don't waste your money on cheap "alpha" devices or expensive programs promising quick miracles. Rather, if you are seriously interested in exploring biofeedback, introductory courses are often available through adult schools and the like. Also, you might consider one of the relatively inexpensive GSR (galvanic skin resistance) systems now on the market. Some can be purchased that have the capability to also measure changes in skin temperature, which might be a worthwhile option for the slight added cost.

Strategies for Learning Psychosomatic Skills

Psychosomatic self-control, then, involves learning new ways of consciously exploiting your natural mind-body linkages. The key to these skills is goal-directed imagining (Key Technique Eight). In fact, the technique you have already been taught can be highly effective for working with your psychosomatic responses.

However, there are many times when that approach is impractical or inappropriate. More than that, goal-directed imagining is a general approach; you will want to learn some actual ways of going about doing psychosomatic self-control. You want something to do, not something to think about.

Therefore, you will also need to learn how to develop and work with *structured routes*—standardized exercises you can do in the same way you do your basic self-hypnosis. In application, however, structured routines serve like informal self-hypnosis techniques. Both are designed for using on the spot to bring about a specific, desired effect.

To master psychosomatic self-control skills, then, you should take into account the following considerations:

1. *Work within formal self-hypnosis when exploring new objectives or learning new tactics.* Self-hypnosis can only facilitate successful psychosomatic control. Biofeedback equipment would also be appropriate at this stage. However, you may find working in this formal context too cumbersome for pragmatic, on-the-spot use.

2. *Release any mental or physical tensions and blockages by relaxing completely before engaging in thinking, feeling, and imagining to create the desired psychosomatic responses.* Once you are familiar with eliciting psychosomatic response, you can usually skip this preliminary. However, if ever you should find yourself blocked or unable to get into the psychosomatic control technique, then go back and begin again with complete relaxation.

3. *Train yourself with goal-directed imagining.* This is your key to attaining psychosomatic self-control. Relaxation and/or self-hypnosis potentiates its effects, but this is the basis of all your psychosomatic techniques.

4. *For on-the-spot or everyday use, consider learning a structured routine.* Goal-directed imagining will always work (if anything can or will), but train yourself to also work with a standardized procedure as a practical shortcut.

5. *Once you are familiar with eliciting or shaping psychosomatic response through a structured routine, you can further condense it into a cue tactic.* As we'll discuss, you can select a word, phrase, or set of actions you would not normally say or do in everyday life and then train yourself to trigger the series of psychosomatic actions or events

required to bring about the total desired response. In this fashion, you need not devote nearly so much time, effort, or attention to things you will be doing again and again in daily life.

6. *Always incorporate an immediate sensory component in your cues and, if appropriate, in structured routines.* This trick was explored in Chapter Six with regard to your standardized self-hypnosis exercise; the tactic of touching a finger to your forehead to begin was really an example of a cue being used to trigger the induction process.

7. *It is generally advisable to close your eyes and/or use the zero technique as the beginning of your structured routines and immediately before giving yourself any other cue.* This trick takes no more than seconds, while enormously facilitating response to your own intentions and imaginations.

8. *Whatever strategems you devise, make them simple—but also make them something you can comfortably work with.* Use any or all tricks in the book. The right technique is one that works for you when you need it.

The remainder of this chapter will be devoted to applying these principles to actual psychosomatic objectives. I will provide guidelines and examples for doing this kind of work, but only you can select an approach that's right for you. I will show you at least one visualization, structured routine, and cue tactic for each sort of task. First, though, let's consider an overall plan of action by which you can address any or all tasks of psychosomatic self-control.

Key Technique Sixteen: Program for Psychosomatic Self-Control
Use

> As your overall strategy and plan of action for learning, mastering, applying, and eventually making a habit or reflex of doing psychosomatic self-control with regard to any particular need, skill, or objective.

Method

Your basic strategy is broken down into a sequence of seven steps or stages. Work with each stage until you feel comfortable with it and can get some effect from it. Then go on to learn the next stage of proficiency. In practice, depend primarily upon the last stage you have already mastered, going back to an earlier stage if necessary to get the desired effect while on the spot.

Directions

*1. *Visualize in self-hypnosis.* Begin with goal-directed imagining in part nine of your basic routine. Once you feel good about it, go on to the next step.

2. *Imagine yourself doing the structured routine, still visualizing in self-hypnosis.* Now rehearse using the structured routine with great success, but in your imagination only. You might want to combine this with step 1—first do the goal-directed visualization, and then immediately imagine going through the routine with great success.

*3. *Actually go through the structured routine within self-hypnosis.* You can substitute this for suggestion and visualization or do in part nine. Here, you are still using the self-hypnosis format to facilitate response.

*4. *Use the structured routine by itself.* Begin actually practicing using your routine to elicit the desired effects outside of self-hypnosis.

5. *Visualize working with a cue in self-hypnosis.* In your daily self-hypnosis practice, begin imagining yourself working successfully with a cue alone. This is a training step just like step 2.

*6. *Use the cue by itself.* Begin practicing using the cue to trigger desired responses as your primary technique in daily life, for on-the-spot use. Remember, for this to work you must (a) involve your imagination and (b) allow it to work for you.

*7. *Begin to just do it.* Once you've learned to routinely bring about desired psychosomatic responses with a cue, you will no longer need a cue or anything else. The *intention* alone can trigger the most complex responses now, if you (a) imagine that it will and (b) allow yourself to respond.

This last stage is where you want eventually to end up—able to bring about the desired response by just intending it to occur for you. Now it is truly yours, something you can do almost automatically, a habitual routine. The ultimate stage of psychosomatic self-control does away with the whole quality of *control*; your body simply responds to your needs and desires.

Note: Each step marked with an asterisk (*) can serve to bring about the desired response when you need it.

Using Good Sense

To make things go right for yourself, it is absolutely essential that you use good sense. It's not that you shouldn't try for your dreams. You cannot do the impossible, of course—but who knows what is or is not possible? If you need a miracle, why not give it your best shot?

There is, in fact, evidence suggesting that goal-directed imagining and related strategies can actually affect the course of such horrendous problems such as terminal cancer. The renowned oncologist O. C. Simonton reports exciting preliminary findings indicating that some of his patients have been able to raise their body's resistance to the spread of cancer and may even have achieved total remissions through this kind of visualization practice. His methods remain unproven, but if you are faced with a problem like terminal cancer, the only crazy thing is not to try to do something about it.

By all means take charge of your own wellness and

don't depend on the medical or any other establishment to do it for you. Do the very best for yourself. What good sense means in this context is making sure that you really are doing the best for yourself.

Seek professional diagnosis and treatment for serious injuries or illnesses, new or chronic pains, severe emotional and other classically "psychological" difficulties, etc. Taking charge of your life and health implies using common sense—and it is only good sense to seek expert help when you need it. It's far better to learn that you don't need treatment than not to have caught a problem until too late.

With this understanding, you can safely work toward psychosomatic self-management and perhaps even accomplish a few miracles for yourself. This is one of the last frontiers of our human potential, so keep an open mind and learn what you can accomplish on the principle *you never know—so why not?*

Warming Yourself by Suggestion

Cognitive control over blood flow and, therefore, body temperature was one of the first psychosomatic self-control skills to be scientifically investigated and verified. You neither have to be a yogi nor be hypnotized to do this. You experience this psychosomatic effect on an involuntary basis in daily life when you blush or blanch, and, of course, in sexual arousal. However, research has now shown that any normal person can gain a meaningful degree of control over body temperature and blood flow on a voluntary basis, in a relatively brief time, and without any great difficulty.

The secret is using goal-directed imagining combined with an attitude of allowing yourself to respond. Warming yourself by suggestion is more than an academic exercise. This skill can be used for an enormous variety of practical objectives: warming parts of your body that feel cold to you, keeping your entire body warm in cold environments, promoting the healing of wounds and other injuries by increasing blood supply to the affected area, shrinking warts and tumors by restricting blood supply to a specific area, enhancing sexual response, controlling migraine headache, relieving joint and muscle pain, etc.

Key Technique Seventeen: A Model Psychosomatic Strategy (Warming Yourself)

Use

To illustrate how one goes about using self-control skills in actual practice, working with the example of warming yourself by suggestion.

Method

A. *Visualization in Self-Hypnosis.* Use goal-directed imagining as appropriate.

Examples: Picture yourself soaking up heat in a warm bath or hot tub, or warming your hands by an open fire; imagine the sun warming your body. To facilitate response, you may use biofeedback equipment and/or other mechanical aids such as dipping your hand in warm or hot water while imagining that it is becoming warm. This trick does not have to be limited to your initial training period—use it whenever it can help.

B. *Structured Routine.* Here is an example of a structured routine for warming yourself which can be adapted to many other psychosomatic applications.

Examples: Practice this sequence of steps. Once you are familiar with them, it will go really fast.

1. Close your eyes, take a deep breath, and say "zero."
2. Now imagine making one hand warm, holding your breath if possible. Hint—once you've learned to warm your hand with a detailed goal-directed fantasy, you can just zip through the same basic imagining and trigger an identical effect in almost no time flat. Therefore, use a fantasy you've trained yourself to work with in self-hypnosis.
3. Touch this hand to your cheek, visualizing that all its

real or imagined warmth is draining out of the hand and deep into your cheek as you exhale or blow out. *It does not matter what you are actually feeling as yet, just imagine you can feel the desired warmth; pretend or make believe and it will actually happen in due course.*

4. Now withdraw your hand from your cheek, while imagining that you can actually feel the warmth becoming stronger and more realistic in your cheek.

5. Then touch your hand again to your cheek, this time as you inhale, and imagine sucking all the warmth—real and imagined—back into your hand. *Imagine that with every transfer you can feel this warmth intensifying.*

6. In this fashion, repeat steps 3 to 5 over and over for as long as you'd like, allowing the feeling and/or imagination of warmth to grow stronger and stronger for you.

7. Now touch your "warm" hand to any or all parts of your body where you wish to increase temperature or blood supply, as you blow out; imagine the warmth draining through any clothing, skin, or flesh into the precise area where you want it to go. It can and will if you let it. Repeat for all areas you wish to warm.

8. Withdraw your hand, take another deep breath, and open your eyes. Now allow yourself to feel as if you can actually feel the warmth, and continue doing whatever you should be doing. Note: There may be a few seconds' or minutes' time lag between when you do this and when you experience actual objective warmth. Don't worry—trust yourself. It will happen if you imagine it will happen and then allow it to happen. The more you practice, the longer-lasting, quicker, and easier to achieve will be the desired effects.

C. *Cue Tactics.* Once you can get somewhere with your

structured routine, teach yourself to work with a cue. While many hypnotists work with verbal cues ("When I say the word *bumbershoot*, you will return immediately to deep hypnosis"), more and more have come to appreciate the value of sensory cues (rather than a word, using a touch on the left shoulder for instant induction). You'd do well to also make your cues both meaningful and tangible.

Example: Here's my own routine. To train myself, I spent an hour or so in self-hypnosis by a fireplace in a ski cabin. I sat before the fire and first worked on really getting the scene firmly in my mind; I practiced, with my eyes open, making myself aware of every sensory stimulus I could possibly notice. Once I had firmly established the scene for myself in this way, I stretched my hands out toward the flames, bending them up so my palms faced the fire. I then spent a long while concentrating, with my eyes closed, on the sensations of my hand being warmed by the fire. I observed and recorded in my mind the tingling in my palms, how it grew almost unbearable, etc. Then I withdrew my hands, allowed them to cool, and repeated this ritual of stretching out my hands, bending the palms up, feeling the tingling, etc. I went through this over and over until I felt it was time to end my session.

Now, to warm my hands, I set my mind (telling myself what I'm about to do or merely *intending* that this occur), close my eyes, and bend up my hands so the palms face outward. I open my eyes and can almost instantly observe my palms become blotchy and mottled as the blood flow changes. I can then touch my warmed hand(s) to any other part of my body, intending for the warmth to spread. Sometimes I pass the warmth back and forth to build it up, but this is not often necessary. The whole procedure takes only a few seconds now— that's how simple cue tactics can be!

As you will notice, we have introduced a new concept in this section of the chapter—*intending*. This is the ultimate stage of psychosomatic self-control and any other skills you are using strategic self-hypnosis to learn and master. *Once you have familiarized yourself with doing a certain kind of thing by hypnotic means, it can become something you can just allow yourself to do.* Now, all you have to go through in order to bring about this response or effect is to intend to do it. This is just like what you do when thinking; you don't have to go through the whole process of actually speaking the words, you just *intend* to do so and you experience the word in your mind. Sarbin calls this "muted, attenuated speech." I'd call it the *intention* to speak.

Experiment Twenty: Warming Yourself
Purpose

To explore working with visualization and a structured routine for self-regulation of body temperature and blood flow, in order to gain familiarity with strategies of psychosomatic self-control.

Method

Self-hypnosis with cue cards.

Directions

Prepare two cue cards. To do so, first go over Key Technique Seventeen to familiarize yourself with the methods involved. Then, on one card, write *One*, below this write *goal-directed visualization*, and under that, suggest a theme to work on that would involve your hand becoming very warm. Focus on your right hand if right-handed, your left hand if left-handed. Your entire body can be warmed in your visualization, but we are most interested in the one hand for this experiment.

On the second card write *Two*, under that, *structured routine*, and then something to remind yourself what to do. For example, you might put *1-zero, 2-warm, 3-touch, 4-withdraw, 5-touch again & repeat.* For this experiment you don't need to use steps 7 and 8, although if there is some part of your body you'd like to begin working on warming, add this to the visualization and also add steps 7 and 8 to your cue card. After a few times, you'll not need a cue card for this routine, but at least have one available this first time through.

You will want to do this experiment in at least three sessions over the next few days. After your first time through, go on reading in this chapter.

For the first session, do your full basic self-hypnosis routine to part nine, with your card labeled *One* at hand if you need it. When you have completed visualization of your formula, say a few zeros and then go through a goal-directed fantasy for warming your hands and any other parts of your body. Really build it up as a realistic experience. Whenever you're ready, end your session as you normally would. In your journal note how it went, any clear results, any problems.

If you had a difficult time with the hand-warming visualization, work with a basin of hot water beside you in your next session; as you imagine the hand becoming warmer, dip it into this hot water and focus on feeling it actually becoming warmer. If you have access to biofeedback apparatus equipped to respond to warmth, that would also be a great aid. If you had no problems with your visualization, these supplementary measures are entirely optional.

The next time you would do a self-hypnosis session in your daily routine, do your second part of this experiment. Have your cue cards stacked in order, as in earlier experiments, and go through your routine to part nine. Open your eyes and glance at the first card. Close your eyes, say a few zeros, and again do a goal-directed imagination for hand warming. Use supplementary aids as you'd like. Immediately upon ending your visualization, open your eyes and read over the second card, reminding yourself of the directions for your structured routine. Close your eyes, say a few zeros, and then *in your imagination only* visualize yourself going through these steps with excellent results. End the session and make notes as before.

The next time you would give yourself a session, you can do the third step of this experiment. However, if you are not yet comfortable with the goal-directed imagining procedure, you might want to hold off and repeat the second step immediately above with each of your routine sessions until you do feel ready. There is no rush; just fit this into your normal self-hypnosis schedule.

When you are feeling good about working in visualization, prepare your cue cards as before and give yourself a full self-hypnosis session to part nine. As earlier, using the cue card and any supplementary tricks you'd like, do a goal-directed visualization for warming yourself. You can include within it an imaginative rehearsal of yourself going through the structured routine with good results. Complete your visualization, say "zero" a few times, look over your cue card for the structured routine if you'd like, and this time actually go through the structured routine. End your session and take some notes.

This completes your experiment. At this time, think back over your progress in self-control of body temperature and make some notes and observations for yourself in your journal.

You should already be able to use this skill to warm your hands, feet, or other body parts at need. However, you will want to develop your skill further. Therefore, in your next three or four routine self-hypnosis sessions, do exactly what you did for the third step—visualization and then the structured procedure in part nine of your basic self-hypnosis. This should take no more than a minute or two each time you do it.

Then continue to practice your structured routine in your daily self-hypnosis. At least once a day just go through your structured routine in part nine of the session. If you need to warm yourself, you can begin just giving yourself a self-hypnosis induction and then, skipping the formula and so forth, go directly to the structured routine. After a week or so, you can just begin to use the structured routine by itself when you need it. It would be helpful to continue practicing—say, once a week—in your routine self-hypnosis.

If you find a lot of use for this or any routine, go on to the cue stage. To begin, do exactly as in step two of your experiment, adding rehearsal of the cue. Then do step three and follow the directions of the last two paragraphs.

Controlling Pain

Probably the best-known psychosomatic application of hypnosis is controlling pain. Some subjects become so adept at this that they can undergo major surgery without chemical anesthesia. Many more can learn to have dental work without novocaine.

Whatever your past experiences with pain, with practice your pain-control skills will improve. Even if you don't prove to be one of the rare individuals who is a good candidate for drug-free surgery, you should be able to relieve pains, aches, and discomforts by hypnotic techniques at least as well as you can by over-the-counter medications. Most likely, you can learn to do better than that.

In working with pain, it is important to distinguish

pain from *sensation.* Pain is essentially your response or reaction to sensations perceived to be hurting, intolerable, unbearable, or overwhelming. Your body manages such perceptions biochemically, manufacturing its own narcotic-like substances, called *endorphins,* to block or reduce pain-triggering signals from reaching your brain. However, research evidence seems to indicate that hypnosis works at a different level altogether.

Pain control by suggestion involves asserting your power not to bother to respond in robot fashion, to refuse to become a victim of sensations. With these techniques you learn to alter your perception of potentially painful sensations so they don't bother you. *You can either keep your attention off the source of pain, ignore the sensations, or redefine them to mean something other than pain.*

You've done this already in daily life. There were times something hurt and other times when the same thing did not bother you. When you are preoccupied, for example, you can ignore or not be aware of receiving minor injuries or experiencing discomfort.

By strategic self-hypnosis, you can learn to place this ability under your voluntary control. Three strategies are most useful for this purpose: relaxation, distraction, and goal-directed imagining. These can be used alone or in any combination.

Relaxation is your first line of defense against pain. Barber and other researchers have shown that there is a mutually antagonistic relationship between pain and relaxation. *The more tense you are, the more you hurt; the more relaxed you are, the less the same things pain you.* This is why relaxation can be so important in controlling your perception of pain.

For example, relaxation is the basic secret to natural childbirth. Childbirth places a woman in more stress and under more heavy sensations than almost anything else she could possibly experience. However, as millions of prepared mothers have learned, childbirth need not be a matter of agonizing, unbearable pain.

This was first realized by a British obstetrician, Dr. Grantley Dick-Reade, the father of natural childbirth. He discovered that simply reducing fear and anxiety by educating the prospective parent in the facts of the birthing process eliminated most of the pain associated with having babies. Lamaze techniques added a variety of psychosomatic techniques, including progressive relaxation, to better promote "childbirth without pain."

However, a newer approach called the Bradley Method is even more exciting, both in its excellent results and because it involves nothing more strenuous than deep relaxation practiced throughout the labor. It is the ultimate in allowing the woman to work *with* her body to facilitate the most joyous or even spiritual childbirth possible.

The Bradley Method also illustrates how deep relaxation can be combined with visualization for the very best results obtainable. Involving your imagination both gives you something to do about what's happening, and apparently allows you to help things along; it has both symbolic and practical value. Many Bradley mothers, for instance, visualize their contractions as ocean waves flowing through their bodies, opening up the birth canal wider and wider.

Your second basic strategy is *distraction.* In this approach, you concentrate on something else so that you aren't noticing or placing any great importance upon those aspects of your situation that might otherwise give you pain. Two varieties of distraction are most commonly employed for this purpose: *thinking about something else* (than what is actually going on right now), and *putting yourself imaginatively into a different scene or situation.*

The first tactic can work like a charm for some

people, and for just about anybody some of the time. However, it involves considerable effort and self-discipline. This requirement often makes this tactic impractical in the actual situation. The second approach, not using anything like willpower, can work where the first cannot.

Furthermore, it provides all the benefits of using a visualization strategy, discussed in this volume, even while it builds on everything you have been learning about using your imagination. What you want to do to distract yourself is *create a visualization of a place, time, or situation in which you might rather be and within which pain would be the last thing on your mind.* Then get yourself into that scene using the techniques you have learned for effective visualization.

Many people prefer a relaxation scene, imagining something from memory or making up a wish-fulfillment fantasy. You worked with this kind of visualization back in Experiment Eleven.

Others prefer a more active sort of make-believe adventure, usually coupled with physical pleasure and imagination of total involvement in the make-believe reality. For example, a client reported that he had previously experienced great success with this tactic. During major dental surgery, he had visualized himself, his girlfriend, and (this was *his* fantasy) Jesus Christ drinking beer and having a grand time on a yacht in the middle of San Francisco Bay. By really getting into this fantasy, he was able to go through the procedure without novocaine or other drugs, to which he happened to be allergic.

The third strategy is another application of *goal-directed imagining.* You create a fantasy which would be incompatible with, prevent, or in some other fashion not allow you to feel pain. The other two strategies are most applicable when you can do nothing else but concentrate on doing them—as during dental work, recuperating from surgery or illness, or other times when you can be inactive and "out of it." The third strategy can be used, like your hand-warming technique, on the spot and at times when you need to relieve pain or discomfort while remaining active, alert, and able to deal with your environment.

Because you can transfer this strategy to a structured routine or cue, it is your method of choice for everyday use and to replace minor pain relievers like aspirin. It is also the method used, normally in combination with relaxation, for drug-free surgery and with intractable pain in lower-back injuries, terminal cancer, etc.

Selection of what to imagine is, as always, entirely up to you. Barber, for example, likes to use an imagination of novocaine making the body part numb. Other clinicians prefer the fantasy of becoming numb from the cold. I have had good results as well from totally off-the-wall visualizations like picturing two pipes running between my brain and my hand, one of which is the "pain pipe," which alone carries nerve messages regarding pain from my hand to my brain. This pipe is ugly mustard yellow. The other pipe, blue, carries all other impulses between hand and brain— but it cannot carry pain signals at all. To turn off the pain, I imagine shutting a valve on the pain pipe, closing it off completely. Then I build up the anesthesia or numbness in my hand exactly as we build up the warmth in Key Technique Seventeen.

This last example brings out the crucial point that *you can use the general pattern of Key Technique Seventeen for nearly all psychosomatic goals, just as you can train yourself to use practically all psychosomatic techniques with the strategies of Key Technique Sixteen.* Once you master these two approaches, you have the wherewithal to achieve all forms of psychosomatic self-control.

Again, however, I must stress the point of using good sense. Always get new pains of unknown meaning or origin checked out before you attempt to get rid of them by suggestion (although you can certainly reduce their discomfort while awaiting diagnosis if you let your doctor know exactly how it felt before you did so). Of course, if you are a victim of chronic or intractable pain that has already been medically checked out, feel free to reduce or entirely rid yourself of it by self-hypnotic means. Similarly, if you are on routine heavy doses of painkillers for migraine, arthritis, or other chronic conditions, there is no reason to not replace the medications with your own imagining. In such a case, it is preferable to discuss the situation with your doctor.

Another important point about working with pain is that *your choice of visualization can have a direct, rather than merely symbolic, effect upon the effectiveness of pain control.* For example, where the medical treatment would be application of heat—as in muscle aches, inflammation, or joint pain—you can only improve matters by selecting a warming theme. On the negative side, I would not advise you to use a fantasy which would withdraw blood supply and energy from the affected area if there is a wound or surgical incision needing to be healed. In such cases, imagining becoming numb from the cold would be counter-productive.

Alternatively, you can select a visualization with no likely direct consequences. The "shutting off the pain pipe" fantasy described earlier was of this sort. Another would be to imagine taking a drug that you know would work or, better yet, which you have actually experienced relieving the kind of pain you are dealing with. This is the logic behind Barber's use of novocaine.

The traditional method for hypnotic pain relief is known as glove anesthesia. For this, you use a visualization in which one hand becomes numb—typically from extreme cold. Then you build this numbness up and transfer it to the part(s) of your body requiring relief by the identical routine to that of Key Technique Seventeen.

The suggestions used by most hypnotists for this purpose involve your hand becoming so numb as to feel as if there is a thick leather glove over it, hence the name glove anesthesia.

Why don't most professionals tell the subject their hands will be totally numb so that they could feel no sensation at all? Because that (a) rarely ever happens even if suggested, and (b) if successful, would in effect sever the subject's hand from his or her body. Therefore, when inducing hypnotic anesthesia, you still want to be able to perceive pressure and and all non-pain sensations—*be smart and permit such feelings within your goal-directed visualization.*

Since controlling pain represents a modification of the techniques already presented in this chapter, let's experiment with this psychosomatic skill. If you are still working with the last experiment, that's okay. Take a break and try this one.

Experiment Twenty-One: Specific Pain Relief
Purpose
> To explore how the techniques you have been learning can be adapted to control, reduce, or completely eliminate pains and aches.

Method
> Self-hypnosis with cue cards.

Directions
> Prepare two cue cards. On the first, write *One*, below that *goal-directed visualization*, and underneath that line suggest your theme. Label the second card *Two, structured routine,* and then indicate the steps: *1—zero, 2—numb, 3—touch, 4—withdraw, 5—touch again & repeat, 6—pinch to check.* As before, include steps 7 and 8 of Key Technique Seventeen if you wish to focus on a specific painful area of your body, and include relieving that area in the visualization.
>
> For visualization themes, I'd suggest beginning with the idea of numbness either from local anesthesia

or from the cold. For the latter, you might imagine playing in the snow, or plunging your hand into ice water or brine like that once used to keep beer and soft drinks cold in old-time markets. If you'd prefer something more imaginative, you could pretend that it's not really your hand but a fake rubber hand from a joke shop, or the hand of a department store mannequin. Again, select whatever kind of visualization you can feel comfortable with.

The "check" step on your second card refers to this: Once you have made your hand seem numb, you will reach over with your free hand and pinch it until you can't feel the pinch any longer. Then you know you are doing it—this is a crude form of biofeedback. Once you can no longer feel any pain from your pinch, only pressure and other dull sensations, let go and return your other hand to your lap or your side and continue. To get the idea right now, take your *left hand* (if you are right-handed, right hand if left-handed) and pinch the top of your other hand so you can really feel the pain. Then stop hurting yourself!

To do the experiment, you will shortcut the full training procedure of Key Technique Sixteen, although you would probably want to go through the full procedure if you have any great difficulty. In fact, once you've worked with the full training sequence as in your last experiment, you can usually start working with new self-control applications as follows.

Have your cue cards stacked in order beside you. Close your eyes and set your mind, telling yourself what you are about to do and how you would like to do it. Now go through your basic self-hypnosis routine to part nine. Open your eyes and read your first cue card, close your eyes and say a few zeros, then build your visualization. Once you've really developed the feeling of numbness, open your eyes again and look at your second card, which lists the steps of the structured routine. Close your eyes, say a few zeros, and imagine going through the steps of this procedure with fantastic results. Open your eyes and again review your card, if you must, or else just say a few more zeros and then go through the actual procedure, including the pinch test. As you pinch your hand, imagine the numbness building. When you've made certain you can't feel any pain from the pinch any longer, simply end your session at this point, or transfer the numbness to any part of your body where you'd like it to go and then end your session. Open your eyes and make your notes.

To train yourself in this application of psychosomatic self-control, begin by doing this same thing during routine self-hypnosis. Wait, of course, till you've done all you want to do with the hand warming from our last experiment. Then, at least daily, go through this same routine a few more times, perhaps skipping the visualization of doing the technique, or better still, just imagine doing it very quickly at the end of your visualization. Once you feel ready, begin just practicing the routine in part nine of your basic daily sessions. Proceed as directed in Experiment Twenty. Maintain your various self-control skills by running through each procedure you have learned at least once a week in conjunction with your routine self-hypnosis.

Working with pain relief is best done when you are not in pain. Prepare yourself for the real thing in imaginative rehearsal, before you are called upon to actually handle pain. Then you will be in the best shape to do so. Of course, if you are troubled by chronic pain already this would not be feasible. However, in such a case, I'd advise you to work a little harder at relaxing yourself completely during the self-hypnotic induction.

Other self-control objectives can also be achieved by

modifying the basic approach from Key Techniques Sixteen and Seventeen. Always obtain medical clearance or consult an alternative professional of your choice if you wish to work with a potentially serious physical problem or condition. Don't expect too much support from the average physician or other provider—the idea is still too novel for many professionals to accept it. However, use your own judgment— *so long as there is no reason not to go ahead with psychosomatic self-control strategies, you might as well.*

It you need to be treated professionally, of course get yourself taken care of. Then work to help yourself along. If you're told there is nothing they can do or that everything has already been done, then set to work on your self-hypnosis program.

Self-hypnosis and related tactics of suggestion have been used with at least some success for the widest range of medical and psychosomatic problems or conditions. These include improving eyesight, obtaining relief from hiatal hernia, relaxing jaw muscles to combat tooth grinding or gag reflex, relieving eczema and other dermatological conditions, healing injuries and surgical wounds, controlling asthma and other allergies, overcoming colds and other minor ailments, relieving back pain, and, of course, relaxation in childbirth.

Psychosomatic Self-Management

Two other psychosomatic endeavors are more like self-management than self-control. For *healing* and *promoting wellness,* you can adopt an approach in which you use a formula appropriate to the goal and work with it in your daily self-hypnosis. Remembering the future is particularly well adapted to this purpose.

Especially as you age or your physical condition deteriorates, you might find these goals become most important to you. While there is less scientific evidence for achieving either by self-hypnosis, there is more than enough to suggest that you'd do well to give it a go and find out how much you can actually accomplish.

For healing, you want to select an appropriate self-hypnosis formula and then visualize it coming true or having already come true. As an added tactic in part nine, or as part of the basic visualization, you might imagine a glowing healing energy or force at work in your body. Add sounds, colors, and feelings that can symbolize this for you. White or golden light, religious or spiritual sounds, feelings of warmth, tingling and energy in your body, have all been suggested for this purpose.

Work in a similar fashion when striving toward positive wellness. Perhaps visualize yourself remembering back to how you achieved a state of robust health and positive well-being as you made your formula come true. A healing-energy visualization or imagining yourself being filled with life energy could be helpful, as would seeing yourself in your mind's eye being youthful, hearty, physically fit, and everything else you desire to be.

These are by their very nature long-term goals. They differ in this respect from the other psychosomatic objectives we've discussed previously. However, this kind of project is certainly worth exploring if you are recuperating from illness or injury, to combat negative effects of aging or disease processes, or if you simply feel committed to motivate yourself to develop a life-style, mental attitude, and other habits conducive to optimal well-being.

TEN

Programs for Maximum Performance

In this final chapter we'll consider how you can put together a total program for improving your performance in every area of your life. Illustrating how you can use the principles and techniques in this volume to facilitate maximum performance, we will consider how to go about improving sports and other manual or public performances, and also how to strategize toward improvement in primarily intellectual performance in study, taking tests, and similar situations.

Advanced Techniques

Before we do that, however, we need to go over two advanced techniques belonging in your repertoire of hypnotic skills. There are many times, for example, when you want the concentration, freedom from distraction, and facilitation of learning and recall you can get from self-hypnosis, but when you do not want to be relaxed or otherwise "out of it." Especially in performance situations, you may want all the benefits of hypnosis, but in such a way that you can remain wide awake, with your eyes open.

Because you have learned to enter a hypnotic frame of mind through repeated practice of your basic routine, you can now begin to explore the possibilities of *waking hypnosis*. All I mean by this term is doing self-hypnosis without deeply relaxing yourself and while remaining wide awake in every way. This will not replace your routine practice, but it provides a useful alternative for times when becoming completely relaxed and focusing on your imaginations would be inappropriate.

Key Technique Eighteen: Waking Self-Hypnosis
Use

Whenever you want the benefits of a hypnotic frame of mind while remaining wide awake, with your eyes open.

Method

Waking self-hypnosis routine.

Directions

Parts 1, 2, 3, and 4 of your basic self-hypnosis routine are the same. However, you do not repeat "zero" over and over after saying it the first time. Rather, after you say "zero" as you exhale, do the following:

4a. Set your mind—tell yourself what you are going to do in your waking self-hypnosis and exactly how you want this to be done. Then briefly visualize doing it in that way.

5a. Open your eyes and set to work.

6a. When you are done, it is strongly advisable to close your eyes, review what you have accomplished, tell yourself a suggestion (either your formula or a special suggestion concerning whatever you are working on in waking hypnosis), and count yourself up just as in your basic routine. *Make a point of always formally ending every session of self-hypnosis, waking or not, and you can't go wrong.*

Another advanced technique is making up your own tapes. You have been doing this throughout this book, only now you will work with your own scripts. You already know how to record tapes for yourself, so we primarily need to cover how to organize your scripts and effectively work with the tapes.

When making up your own tapes, you will normally begin with some kind of induction procedure. You could simply use parts 1–5 of your basic self-hypnosis routine, or take the induction portion from any of the session scripts you have worked with. You can, of course, also make up your own. A minimal induction would consist of some suggestions for relaxation, perhaps a visualization for relaxing and letting go, and would also include some suggestions to provide positive expectations for yourself, such as how well it will go.

Many hypnosis practitioners like to provide from one to ten minutes of silence immediately after the induction procedures, to allow you to settle into a hypnotic frame of mind. I normally employ a brief silent period, as in your scripts, during which I often would have you do something like say "zero" or squeeze and relax your eyes. Experiment with this tactic of silence on your own—to start, I'd suggest you try two to five minutes. You can, by the way, play soothing, dreamy, or "hypnotic" music or sounds—softly—in the background during this time. I've had good success with sound effects like the ocean or the sounds of a mother's womb.

After the silent period, begin the body of your session. Follow the rules you have learned concerning the strategic approach. Rely primarily on visualizations. However, when using a tape, you can do a lot more with verbal suggestions than when giving yourself the basic self-hypnosis session. Use symbols, indirect tactics, and, especially, extensive narration to prompt your imaginings.

One tactic you can use to great benefit on your tapes but not in other self-hypnosis is *commenting to yourself.* Here you can really put to work the defining function of verbal suggestions. What you do is to intersperse comments defining the situation within the flow of your narrative. This requires you to step outside of the imaginary experience to remark upon it—which is why you don't often employ such a tactic in routine self-hypnosis. You can see this tactic of commenting used in all the session scripts supplied in this book; for example, when you find the comment "It feels so good to be free" in the middle of suggestions prompting you to visualize yourself doing something.

Whether you should use the first person (*I* and *me*) to address yourself, or the second person (*you*), is entirely a matter of what you feel most comfortable with. You have worked with both in your session tapes. It is normally easier to record a tape when using the second person, since we naturally speak to another this way, but some people will prefer to use *I* and *me*. Experiment with both, or look back in your journal and see if one or the other worked better for you.

How long should your tapes be? I'd suggest that you use one side of a 60-minute cassette, making your session between 20 and 30 minutes long. This is about the length of the sessions in this volume. Many practitioners like sessions 15 to 20 minutes in length, although in my own practice, I used mostly 45-minute sessions. It has been my experience that most people do best at home with sessions of the length I have suggested, although you can use even shorter sessions as you deem appropriate.

You can use your tapes to supplement your self-hypnosis routine. They can be particularly valuable as a reinforcement, or when you bog down in your self-management or other work. Tapes offer an excellent way to start working toward new objectives or with new techniques. They also allow you to get more deeply involved than you would in your regular self-hypnosis. Tapes can also be of great value when you are working to deal with specific problems, performances, or other objectives in the near future.

T. X. Barber suggests an entirely different and more radical way of using your own tapes. You might like to explore a version of his approach adapted for use with this volume. An alternative form of self-hypnosis practice, this exploits the interesting fact that you can drastically alter your subjective sense of time's passage in hypnosis so that you can experience a half hour's session in a minute or two by using hypnotic imagining. In Exercise Thirteen, for example, you imagined an episode lasting hours and hours in less than 30 minutes of real time.

Key Technique Nineteen: Self-Hypnosis Tapes
Use

As an alternative or supplement to your routine self-hypnosis exercise.

Method

Imagining along with tapes, at least to begin.

Directions

There are two stages to this approach, the second of which is entirely optional, an alternative form of self-hypnosis practice.

1. *Making up your tape.* As discussed in this chapter, you will make up your own session tape. First think out what you want to accomplish or work toward with this session and write out your script, either word for word or in outline or note form. Begin the session with an induction and then develop your themes in the body of the session, being sure to end your tape with counting up and feeling wide awake and wonderful (always include such suggestions in your scripts).

Alternative inductions can include progressive relaxation, going directly to a goal-directed fantasy for deep relaxation, or imagining time slowing down. This last is a favorite of Barber's. An example would be something like this: "Time is slowing down for me now . . . there is more and more time between every beat of my heart . . . more and more time between every new second [you can help yourself by saying this as if time were slowing down—drawing out words and pauses more and more as you read on] . . . time is slowing down to a crawl . . . and there's more and more time . . . all the time I can possibly imagine . . . more and more . . . time . . . between . . . every . . . beat . . . of . . . my . . . heart . . . each new breath comes slower and slower . . . more and more time . . . all the time I need . . . there's more and more time in every moment . . . time is slowing down more and more. . . ." (etcetera)

Then you might prefer to add a period of saying "zero," as in your self-hypnosis. When you wish, begin the body of your session, using lots of visualizations full of sensory details, adding commentary as appropriate, and taking advantage of such tricks as the verbal formulas "more and more" or "as if." Review your session scripts in this volume for examples. When ready, tell yourself how great you will feel and then end the session.

Now listen to your tape, giving yourself a session in this fashion. It can replace one of your routine self-hypnosis sessions. *If you will be using your own tapes primarily as sessions to give yourself, this is all you need to do.* Suggestion: It rarely pays to work with a formal session more than once every other day. Continue to rely upon self-hypnosis for your routine practice.

2. *Informal self-hypnosis.* However, you can now proceed to use your tapes as the first step in mastering Barber's informal self-hypnosis technique. To begin, listen to your own tape as many more times as necessary until you are thoroughly familiar with it. Of course, you can at any time choose to modify the session to make it work better for you. Your first goal, in any case, is to become so familiar with your preferred tape that you can almost do it in your sleep. Remember to keep up your basic self-hypnosis during this period, perhaps

with a new formula consistent with what you're doing in this session.

Once you are thoroughly familiar with your session, you can begin to replace at least some routine self-hypnosis sessions with Barber's technique. What you do is to sit yourself down and go through everything in your tape, but working from memory. Don't play the tape recorder, but simply *imagine hearing the entire tape from start to stop in your head*. Of course, imagine and respond to the script just as if you were hearing an actual tape. The first few times, you might be more comfortable if you had your script or notes before you to refresh your memory (although that will not probably be necessary).

You will probably already notice that you are "listening" to the entire tape in less time than it would have taken to actually play it. What you are doing is slowing down your subjective sense of time (which is why it can be advantageous to include a slowing-down-time imagination in the induction). Now begin just zipping through the imagined tape in superfast time. With practice, you can seem to "replay" the entire tape in a minute or so. This can then become your routine self-hypnosis. *However, you are well advised to practice some form of deep relaxation daily or at least several times a week.* I'd suggest keeping up your skill at using your basic routine by employing it for that purpose.

Programs of Self-Hypnosis

By a "program," I simply refer to an appropriately put together set of tactics by which you can work toward concrete goals or objectives over whatever period of time is necessary for your particular purpose. When developing your program, be sure to take into account the practical dimension and other aspects of the situation discussed with regard to your self-assessment.

The self-assessment should begin any program of self-hypnosis you attempt. You can only organize a strategy to overcome problems and attain your goals if you understand what you are trying to do. In effect, you will design your self-hypnosis program as the last step of assessing the situation—figuring out what you can do about it. Your program should be designed to overcome those barriers to desired performance found in self-assessment, whether or not anybody else would consider them important.

When you are designing your strategy, keep in mind the fact that self-hypnosis cannot give you anything you don't potentially have already. It can only enable you to tap and to mobilize your own innate resources and potentialities, so that you can bring them to bear upon your situation. This is probably the biggest "only" in the entire universe— whatever your goal, there is at least *some* evidence or rationale to suggest that you just might have the power to accomplish it. We simply do not know what a person *cannot* do or accomplish.

If something is within your power, strategic self-hypnosis offers a practicable way to go about attaining it. Follow the basic principles outlined in this volume for working with your thinking, feeling, and imagining as a method for getting what you want out of life. This is, however, a pragmatic approach. It is designed to be adapted to best fit your own personal needs, interests, and style.

There's no magic in it. The magic's in you. This power is not locked away somewhere in your hidden subconscious mind, it's your very self. The magic manifests itself in everything you think and feel and do.

Nine times out of ten, I find that the person who comes for help with the biggest problem is the one whose own strengths are working against him or her. Nine times out of ten, all it takes to unblock yourself is to cease fighting against yourself, learn to control your powers of mind, and get them working with and for yourself instead.

Self-hypnotic strategies offer three main kinds of tactical benefits useful in improving performance and accomplishing your objectives. The first, discussed in considerable detail earlier, is *providing a means for mental and physical relaxation.*

The second is *unblocking and positively facilitating your potential for learning and disciplined performance at both the intellectual and sensorimotor—or feeling—levels.* You will find that your self-hypnosis skills provide an excellent basis for improving performance in sports; in interpersonal situations of every kind; at work; in learning and dealing successfully with tests, examinations, challenges, and crises of every kind.

Third, strategic self-hypnosis gives you the basic tools for letting go and ridding yourself of unwanted habits of thinking, feeling, and acting in your actual daily life. Positively, it gives you a way of acquiring desired habits, improving concentration and memory skills, developing new and better ways of coping with problems and circumstances. *The strategic approach offers an excellent tool for changing and shaping your self and other everyday realities.*

Sports, Manual Skills, and Public Performances

How can you devise a self-hypnosis program to help you achieve maximal performance in sports and other situations where you must physically act? Let's consider the nature of this goal.

The primary barriers to performance, at either the physical or intellectual level, are your old mental and bodily habits, attitudes, tensions, and their manifestations as self-consciousness, anxiety, nervousness, etc. All of these things are potentially under your voluntary control and can be managed by techniques of strategic self-hypnosis.

These boil down to two fundamental problems: your

meanings and your reactions to your own meanings. By learning new ways of doing things and by practicing them in imaginative rehearsal and in the outer world, you can improve your performances of every sort.

Let's consider, as an example illustrating the general approach, how you might actually go about improving your performance in a particular sport. The specifics I will discuss can be adapted easily for other sports and for the performing arts, court reporting, secretarial work, and manual skills of every sort. They also have been reported to be an enormous help in public-speaking situations, sales presentations, etc.

Performance goals involve activity; they are not the sort of thing you would want to do when completely relaxed or not focusing upon the objective situation. For these reasons, you don't perform in what is often described as a state of hypnosis. Rather, you want to remain completely alert, 100 percent there.

However, you will find enormous value in working with tapes and your basic self-hypnosis routine to facilitate learning, training, and conditioning yourself for maximum performance. In actually practicing or rehearsing, you may also find waking hypnosis to be very helpful. If you can use these tactics effectively and give yourself enough time to prepare yourself, when it actually comes to doing it—the performance itself—you will probably need nothing more than just to set your mind and allow yourself to do your very best. This goes for both manual tasks like sports and intellectual endeavors such as study or taking tests.

The basic strategy in sports and similar performance situations is training yourself to remain calm, focused, and free from self-consciousness when on the spot. At the same time, you use your imaginative rehearsal techniques to *make the idea for how you want to manage the performance your taken-for-granted reality,* your expectation for how you will actually perform. Finally, as a theme within both of these, you *prepare yourself to allow yourself to do your very best under actual performance conditions.* Everything you do, you do in order to implement these three principles—they are your route to maximum performance.

As discussed, you'll begin your program for improving performance with a self-assessment. Preferably, go through the assessment process focusing on your performance objectives. At the same time, probe to see if you are really looking at a more general problem or pattern of which those objectives are a part.

For example, a teenaged varsity pitcher came to me for help with his baseball performance. In his self-assessment, he wrote that "nervousness and concentration while participating in sports or any high pressure situation is my problem."

He stated his objectives: "During a baseball game, I would like to be able to come up to bat and not be nervous, and to be able to concentrate on what I am going to do. While pitching, I would like to be able to stand on the mound and not let the yells of the crowd and other players affect my performance and my concentration."

He proved to be an exceptionally insightful young man in that he spontaneously realized that this was really part of a general self-management goal. "I would like to not become nervous at anything I do," he wrote. "If I don't get nervous, then I am sure I can concentrate on the situation. I need more confidence in everything I do, so I can do it to the best of my abilities."

Actually, his was a typical case for anyone seeking to enhance their performance in all areas ranging from a sport to giving sales presentations. The problem is performing before an audience—sometimes even the audience of oneself. *In most cases, your major problem will not be skill, practice, attitude, or know-how, but performance anxiety.* That will be where you find the root of your problem, nine times out of ten; worrying before the event about how you will do and then worrying about how you are doing in the actual situation makes you so tense, nervous, self-conscious, and easily distracted that you could in no way do your very best.

Enhancing your performance, then, begins with applying self-management and problem-solving tactics to your specific case and objectives. You should also consider modifying your basic self-hypnosis routine to better fit your goals.

Many clients have reported good results from substituting another cue for the *zero* repeated in part five of the standard routine. The example was mentioned earlier of a man who did well, first with *birdie* and then *eagle*, in improving his golf. In the years since working with this case, I have come to believe that you'd do better with the following tactic.

When working to enhance performance, replace repetition of zero *with a cue suggesting improvement, such as the word* better. *At the same time, when you repeat your cue—whether* zero *or another word—imagine what you want it to mean for you.* You could either visualize actually performing the way you'd desire, or imagine seeing and hearing the audience or spectators bursting into applause. Just flash an image like this in your mind each time you think or say your cue.

Another modification would be to use a cue card in the way Arons originally suggested. State your performance goal, or even sketch a pictorial representation on the card. Read it over two or three times before beginning your session, and then let your mind dwell upon it as you go through your routine.

You should also consider selecting a formula pertaining to your performance goals. Although I have seen good results with very specific suggestions ("I will keep calm and alert and allow myself to react quickly and accurately to return the ball each time it comes over the net"), I strongly suggest that you select a formula more general than your particular goal. For example, in most performance situations you'd cover all bases with "I can relax and feel confident and allow myself to do my very best in all situations and in everything I do." The teenager mentioned earlier used this suggestion with dramatic benefit.

Then, when you do your visualization, you can focus your mind on exactly what you want to do. Make this an imaginative rehearsal of either the future-memory or seeing-it-coming-true type. Build in all the feelings and sensations you'd want to experience in the actual performance. Also, picture yourself doing (or having done) well in the most difficult circumstances you can realistically imagine. *Don't just visualize success, visualize triumph!*

Always start working toward performance goals as long before you will actually have to perform as possible. Especially if you are nervous about the situation or if it is very important to you, spend extra time working with imagination rehearsal techniques in part nine of your routine. At the very least, during the week prior to your big game or performance, use Key Technique Thirteen once or twice daily. Use the drifting technique as well, whenever you feel like it.

Immediately before an actual game or performance, do self-hypnosis and get really deeply relaxed. This should be done before entering the actual performance situation. Then, just before you are to perform, as it really begins, or before each pitch, serve, or other stage of your performance, set your mind (Key Technique Fifteen) to program what you will do next. Just shut your eyes, remind yourself of how you wish to bring it off, visualize that occurring, open your eyes, and go.

Of course, you can use any or all of your other tactics as appropriate. You will probably find the most use for your zero technique; use it whenever you feel a need to calm yourself or clear your mind during actual performance. This can be integrated into your technique for setting your mind as described earlier.

You will also find much value in waking hypnosis. However, this is primarily used during training and practicing. While there is no reason you *cannot* use it during the actual performance, you will rarely need to do so. What it can do for you is help you concentrate, ease learning at both the intellectual and sensorimotor levels, diminish self-consciousness and distractability. It also helps free your mind from old ideas or habit patterns that can only interfere with optimal performance.

"Keeping Your Eye on the Ball"

To enhance your performance, use the strategy I call "keeping your eye on the ball." This is freely adapted from the practice of a tennis pro and hypnotechnician, Roger Buchanan, who works with his clients on the tennis court.

When, for instance, he is teaching the backhand stroke, he places the client in a form of waking hypnosis. Then he instructs them to simply observe him demonstrate the backhand, but to keep their eyes on the ball, paying attention to nothing else. He asks them to just observe the location, movement, trajectory, spin, and all other features of the tennis ball as he hits it with the racquet and sends it across the net. Then, while they are still in waking hypnosis, he has them practice making the ball do the same thing.

The underlying principle is that you cannot help but observe the total performance. However, you will absorb most of the details peripherally, keeping you from bogging down in all those mechanics. I have found Buchanan's approach to be a simple, enjoyable, and effective way to learn and master performance skills. It can easily be adapted to not only sports but drama, dance, music, and work.

However, I will focus my discussion upon sports at this time. In any sport, contest, game, or similar performance, there is an *objective*, such as getting a golf ball into a cup in the ground. To make this happen, there is an instrumental activity or *means*, such as getting the ball to move in a desired way. How you actually do that is the *mechanics of performance.* This could be the physical activity of swinging the golf club in a certain way, how you grip the handle, how you stand, etc.

Usually, unless you are lucky enough to be able to work with someone like Mr. Buchanan, you will have to pick up the basics in the conventional way. Take a class or other course of instruction for beginners, read a book, or ask a friend to show you the mechanics of performance. Once you have the idea of what to do, you can then employ hypnotic strategies for mastering the activity.

The secret of this method is to focus on the means by which you attain your objective, not the mechanics of performance. This trick is roughly similar to that of focusing upon sensory and contextual details in constructing visualizations.

Many sports are actually organized around doing things with a ball: tennis, golf, baseball, basketball, soccer, racquetball, bowling, etc. Others use some other kind of projectile: archery, hockey, shuffleboard, fly fishing, hunting, target shooting, etc.

Another kind of sports activity involves your body's movement or that of some kind of vehicle: fencing, wrestling, the martial arts, running, racing, skiing, gymnastics, driving, diving, etc. Other kinds of performance than sports also have this structure of an objective, an instrumental means, and mechanical details: dramatic arts, dance, public speaking, playing and singing music, typing, taking dictation, keypunching, etc.

By analyzing the nature of your performance activity and sorting out these three elements, you can develop an effective strategy for enhancing performance. You can go about it as follows.

Key Technique Twenty: Training Strategy for Enhanced Performance
Use

To maximize your ability and ease at learning and mastering sports and performances of every sort.

Method

As a training strategy used in self-hypnosis, waking

self-hypnosis, and objective practice of a performance skill.

Directions

First, analyze the sport or other activity to determine its *objective*, the *means* for attaining that objective, and what are the *mechanics* of performance.

If it is a totally new sport or performance for you, you should obtain some beginner's-level knowledge of its mechanical details, as discussed. You could work directly with this technique, but it would be best to have at least some general idea of the details of how to go about it, the rules of the game, and so forth.

In your *routine self-hypnosis*, begin focusing on the *objective* of performance. Use a formula, visualizations, and rehearsal techniques as already discussed. To maximize benefit, be sure to include visualizing yourself mastering the means as you attain these objectives. In this task, remembering the future is particularly helpful.

You will train yourself outside of your regular hypnosis practice, however. For this, you will want to use your *waking self-hypnosis* technique. There are two stages in training—learning and practicing. You can, of course, go back and forth between one and the other—it is just easier to describe what to do if we distinguish these as two separate things.

For learning, you want to work with a *role model*. If at all possible, watch someone at an advanced or professional level demonstrate how and what to do. You could simply use this training strategy on your own while taking professional instruction. You might "cheat" by studying videotapes or movies, or even by watching weekend sports programs on television that feature the sport you are working with. Attend performances by skilled amateurs or professionals. Watch others more advanced than yourself, or have a friend show you his or her technique. While you observe any of these role models, do the following: (a) put yourself into waking self-hypnosis, and (b) "keep your eye on the ball." That is, *focus your complete attention on the instrumental means of performance.* You cannot spend too much time watching role models. I suggest that, after the performance is over, you then close your eyes and do two things: (a) review, in visualization, the way the professional or advanced performer went through the means to obtain his or her objectives, and then (b) imagine yourself doing the same thing. If you'd like, skip the first part, but always, before ending your waking session, close your eyes and rehearse in your imagination—but again, focusing entirely on the means itself. Visualize yourself doing the same thing as the successful professional or other role model.

This will not, however, substitute for actual practice. You must both condition your body and develop the appropriate physical habits or routines. This can only be done in actual practice. For *practicing,* put yourself into waking hypnosis, set your mind, and then practice the means of performance. For instance, practice making the ball do exactly as a professional makes his or her ball do. Practice over and over for as long as you want and then end your session as instructed. Before counting up, remember to review your progress and visualize yourself doing it correctly. Stress the feeling of doing so more than the abstract idea or picture of doing so.

By combining routine self-hypnosis with hypnotically amplified practice, you tap your fullest resources for learning to maximize performance. When actually on the spot, you should only have to set your mind—close your eyes, perhaps say "zero," tell yourself how you want to perform, visualize yourself doing as you've practiced, open your eyes, and allow yourself to perform as best you can. Follow this method and you will amaze yourself.

Studying and Taking Tests

Studying for and taking tests of all kinds represents another, more intellectual, sort of performing. This is not limited to school or other academic situations, but includes preparing for job interviews, practical examinations, civil service tests—even mastering a system for blackjack or other gambling. The strategies we'll be considering are appropriate for any situation in which you are called upon to memorize, recall, organize, and apply knowledge, reasoning ability, or other know-how.

Once again, your primary enemy is performance anxiety. Tension, self-consciousness, fear of failure, distractions—all can team up to make your mind go blank, cause you to freeze and panic or otherwise block yourself from the performance of which you are capable. In addition, studying and learning present their own difficulties—you must overcome any self-imposed limitations concerning your abilities, change poor study habits, and learn to stop putting things off.

The techniques of strategic self-hypnosis are especially well suited to this kind of situation. There are actually three related objectives involved in the enhancement of intellectual performances.

One is a matter of *better self-management.* You can use routine self-hypnosis and self-management tactics to work on attitude, motivation, self-discipline, and self-definition. This last is particularly important: You must stop blocking yourself in order to function at your intellectual and creative peak. If your problem were primarily one of improving memorization, concentration, self-discipline, or self-image, you could work primarily within your regular practice of self-hypnosis. In that case, you'd select a formula and visualization as appropriate to your particular case or needs.

Secondly, there is a matter of *performance anxiety and fear of failure* with regard to meeting tests and other

challenges, coping with oral interviews and other interpersonal situations, and/or specific examinations or other
performance situations coming up in the near future. This
can be dealt with through your problem-solving techniques,
particularly imaginative rehearsals. You should also incorporate the idea of being able to meet such challenges in
your routine formula visualizations; use, for example, remembering the future with regard to this specific area or
problem situation.

Third, there is a larger context of *developing a
training program and/or a program of study* which can become your routine. Obviously, in order to do well on
academic or professional examinations you need to have
first studied and learned the material. Let's consider a
hypnotically enhanced program of study and test taking
which has helped many of my clients and students.

Key Technique Twenty-One: Study and Test-Taking Program

Use

As a regimen for studying and then taking exams, and
as a model for adaptation to other intellectual performance situations.

Method

An integrated program of study and self-hypnosis.

Directions

There are three parts to such a program.

1. *Routine self-hypnosis.* Work on a daily or twice-daily
   basis with an appropriate formula and visualization.
   For problem areas or forthcoming projects, tests, or
   other performance situations, work with imaginative
   rehearsals or drifting in part nine. Problem areas you
   might work on include self-discipline, memorization, procrastination, making sense out of difficult
   material, and coping with oral interviews or difficult
   projects. Often it is appropriate to approach such

problems through both routine self-management and problem-solving tactics. Optional: You can also make up a tape of your own covering study and problem areas, using it in place of some self-hypnosis sessions as reinforcement or as a booster before exams and other performances.

2. *Organize a study routine.* Follow these guidelines:

A. *Be pragmatic.* Organize yourself to fit your work plan to the actual requirements of the course or whatever; keep slightly ahead of class assignments and do things *now* whenever possible, rather than save things for later.

B. *Break your work into segments of one-half to one hour.* Don't study too long at one stretch.

C. *Feel free to study in waking self-hypnosis.* Some people find this very helpful, others do not; find out for yourself when or if this tactic is for you.

D. *Set a realistic goal for yourself, meet it, and then stop for the day.* You can decide how much to cover or how long to work, either on a day-to-day or routine basis, as you'd like.

E. *After each segment of work, take a 5- or 10-minute break.* Stretch, walk around, talk to somebody, have a snack, take your mind off study. Do self-hypnosis if you'd like.

F. *Periodically, use self-hypnosis for review.* At least weekly, preferably every few breaks or when switching to a new subject and before starting to study after a weekend or other long break, review the material you've covered in part nine of your session. Three techniques are most useful: (1) Let your mind drift along the theme of what you've been studying, (2) imagine seeing or writing an outline of the material on a blackboard (or whatever), or (3) use your notes like a cue card, reviewing them before or during your session and then thinking over the material in your mind's eye.

G. *Never go past something you don't fully understand.* As the scientologists suggest, if you come across a word or concept you don't understand, stop right there. Write it down on a list you should keep for this purpose, and find its definition in your notes, texts, or a dictionary. You can review this list from time to time in order to really fix this material in your mind. This tactic will ultimately speed up your rate of study and keep you from bogging down.

H. *After the end of your day's work, give yourself a thoroughly relaxing self-hypnosis session and then take your mind off study entirely.* Review the day's material during your session, if you'd like, but use it primarily to get relaxed and change your mood. Now enjoy your leisure time—the more you follow this program, the more leisure you'll have (and no reason to feel guilty about enjoying yourself).

3. *Handle the actual test, project, or interview as follows:*
   A. Immediately before entering the actual test situation, *do a brief self-hypnosis session to calm and prepare yourself for maximum performance.* Do it in your car or even a rest room if you have no other place. Include (1) casually reviewing what you've studied or prepared, and (2) a positive imaginative rehearsal. Psych yourself up.
   B. *Before actually beginning, but in the actual test location, set your mind as in Key Technique Fifteen.*
   C. *Before each new question or part of your work or performance, clear your mind and calm yourself with your zero technique.* Use this trick to make a pause for yourself so that you can assess the actual situation and the demands being made of you in the most accurate way possible and then act to meet those demands to the best of your ability.
   D. *Take nothing for granted.* Take special care to read and comprehend each question or instruction, making certain that you understand exactly what is

and what is not being asked. Beware of trick questions, double negatives, or the like.

E. *Trust yourself.* Don't necessarily believe your immediate thoughts or feelings, but first make sure you are aware of what's really going on. Ninety percent of the time, however, if you have prepared well, your first answer or impulse *will* be correct. Allow yourself and your mind to do your very best and pay no attention to how you think you are doing or to anything else that does not directly relate to the question at hand. This will become more and more your natural tendency as you practice these tactics.

Beyond Self-Improvement . . .

We end this volume at the beginning of your adventures with strategic self-hypnosis. You have only begun to explore the unfolding of your true potentialities.

What powers are potentially yours? What are the true limits of your personal abilities? What could you be or do or have or feel if you knew it were possible, knew how to go about it, and could let yourself do so?

What are you, really?

These are the true mysteries left to us, the last and greatest frontier. In this volume, we have kept ourselves to the here and now, to matters of self-improvement. That is a good way to begin. However, your explorations should not end with self-improvement. There lies something beyond that—self-actualization.

Explore ever onward; experiment, discover, learn. Anything you imagine may lie within your reach—not sometime in the distant future, but in this life. You have the power to attain your dreams; may you use it wisely, never forgetting that the key to total performance is to never lose the spirit of play!

Experiment Twenty-Two: Beyond Self-Improvement
Purpose
> As a graduation exercise, to have some fun exploring some of the outer limits of hypnosis.

Method
> Tape and do as a session.

Script
> "I will now close my eyes and allow myself to let go and relax, but this time I can feel myself not getting the least sleepy or drowsy because this time I am taking the other direction into hypnosis ... I am becoming more and more awake ... more and more comfortable and peaceful and wider and wider awake with every breath I breathe in ... more and more conscious ... calm ... empty and still with every breath I breathe out for the rest of this session ... more and more fully conscious ... as if I'm waking up out of a lifelong trance into my full, conscious potential ... I can feel myself waking up inside now, more and more ... breaking out of my shell and spreading my wings ... my glorious, gorgeous butterfly wings of imagination ... feeling the power awakening in me ... feeling myself becoming more and more fully conscious ... new mental power and freedom and energy ... new freedom and aliveness ... feeling more and more alive and awake with every breath I breathe in now ... I can begin to sense something wonderful starting to happen deep inside me ... feeling a wonderful magical energy welling up deep inside me ... spreading out now throughout my body and mind ... wonderful, glowing, radiant life energy ... filling my heart with light ... more and more ... I can let myself almost feel this inner light ... this power ... this aliveness ... as I feel myself unfolding like a flower unfolds its petals to blossom ... I can feel myself unfolding inside ... opening up to my own light ... my own power ...

revealing my inner light now . . . feeling it glowing like a warm, wonderful sun in my heart . . . filling my body and mind up with its radiance . . . so good . . . so alive . . . feeling the brilliance of my inner light spreading throughout my body and mind now . . . filling my skin with joy and light . . . I can feel this light soothing and healing and calming and awakening everything it touches . . . transforming me into brilliant light . . . pure consciousness . . . more and more and more I can feel myself like a star of glowing, dancing, joyous light . . . pure consciousness shining through every pore . . . spreading far beyond my skin now . . . filling the room with light and safety and life and joy. . . .

"And I feel as if I'm floating high above my body . . . glancing down, I see it relaxing down there . . . healing itself . . . enjoying itself as I float higher and higher as if in a wonderful dream of power and joy . . . looking down, I see my body relaxing . . . what a miracle it is! All those billions of little cells working together as one . . . giving me life in this world . . . I see my body with new respect now . . . I wonder at my body . . . such a miracle of life . . . starting right now, I can feel a new respect, a new acceptance and comradeship with my body . . . and I look outward . . . my consciousness fills this room . . . and beyond . . . I feel conscious of the entire earth . . . all life as one . . . life striving toward the infinite . . . a dance of life filling time and space . . . I can feel the earth spinning round and round as it dances in its orbit around the life-giving sun . . . and the sun, it is also dancing . . . slow and stately . . . and all the stars are dancing together . . . the universe is a dance of light and energy and something more . . . and I set myself free for a while. . . ."
(2-minute pause)

"And now I let myself slowly return back to my body and myself . . . bringing with me a new joy and aliveness . . . a wonderful new freedom and power into my everyday life . . . soon I will be ready to open my eyes and experience new calmness, confidence, and power . . . a sense of wonder and zest for living . . . more and more naturally living up toward my fullest potentials . . . allowing myself to perform my very best in all situations, under any and all circumstances . . . using my self-hypnosis techniques so long as I need to use them and whenever I need them I use them and they work for me because I can allow myself to do my very best in everything I do . . . and I discover how much more than I ever dared to dream my very best can be . . . thinking back now to how I felt when I first began working with strategic self-hypnosis, I realize how much progress I have already made in my life [10-second pause] . . . but this was just the beginning . . . I am just now starting to come into my full potential as a successful, fully alive, fully awake, fully able human being. . . .

"When I open my eyes, I will feel something . . . I do not yet know what it will be . . . but when I open my eyes, I will certainly feel it . . . and it will tell me beyond a shadow of a doubt that I am well on my way now . . . it will show me how good it can be to be really alive . . . here I go: I take a deep breath, count up, and open my eyes, feeling how great I can feel when I allow myself to feel my very best (30-second pause) . . . back to normal awareness now, feeling wide awake, comfortable, and refreshed. . . ."

End of script. Congratulations—you have finished your training course in strategic self-hypnosis.

References
and Suggested
Readings

GENERAL BACKGROUND

Theodore X. Barber, Nicholas P. Spanos, and John F. Chaves, *Hypnotism, Imagination and Human Potentialities* (New York: Pergamon, 1974).

William S. Kroger, *Clinical and Experimental Hypnosis*, 2nd ed. (Philadelphia: J. B. Lippincott, 1977).

Theodore R. Sarbin and William C. Coe, *Hypnosis: A Social Psychological Analysis of Influence Communication* (New York: Holt, Rinehart and Winston, 1972).

CHAPTER ONE

Edmond Jacobson, *You Must Relax*, 4th ed. (New York: McGraw-Hill, 1962). A source for progressive-relaxation techniques.

CHAPTER TWO

Gregory Bateson, *Mind and Nature: A Necessary Unity* (New York: E. P. Dutton, 1979). A good introduction to the world.

Herbert Blumer, *Symbolic Interactionism* (Englewood Cliffs, N.J.: Prentice-Hall, 1969). Classic technical presentation of the approach.

Ken Dychtwald, *Bodymind* (New York: Pantheon, 1977). A good presentation of the concept.

Barry Glassner and Jonathan Freedman, *Clinical Sociology* (New York: Longman, 1979). A basic overview of this emerging field and how sociological concepts apply to helping people change.

William S. Kroger and William D. Fezler, *Hypnosis and Behavior Modification: Imagery Conditioning* (Philadelphia: J. B. Lippincott, 1976). The first hundred pages supply good theoretical background for hypnosis, behavior modification, and working with imagery.

Alexander Lowen, *The Language of the Body* (New York: Collier, 1971). A classic presentation of how your body "thinks."

Jerome G. Manis and Bernard Meltzer, eds., *Symbolic Interactionism: A Reader in Social Psychology*, 3rd ed. (Boston: Allyn and Bacon, 1978). The best introduction to this perspective, through well-selected readings.

George Herbert Mead, *Mind, Self, and Society* (Chicago: University of Chicago Press, 1934). Hard to read, but the seminal discussion of the symbolic interactionist approach.

Paul Watzlawick, *How Real Is Real?* (New York: Vintage, 1976). A good, popular discussion of how realities are constructed through communication.

CHAPTER THREE

Theodore X. Barber, *LSD, Marihuana, Yoga, and Hypnosis* (Chicago: Aldine, 1970). How they all work; a somewhat technical discussion.

Barber, Spanos, and Chaves, op. cit. Good, but somewhat technical, presentation of our general perspective, especially Chapters 1–8.

Milton H. Erickson, Ernest L. Rossi, and Sheila Rossi, *Hypnotic Realities: The Induction of Clinical Hypnosis and Forms of Indirect Suggestion* (New York: Irvington, 1976). Case-study introduction to Erickson's methods of indirect suggestion—a good source for tactics and ideas. A tape is available from the publishers to go with this volume.

Erika Fromm and Ronald E. Shor, eds., *Hypnosis: Developments in Research and New Perspectives*, 2nd ed. (New York: Aldine, 1979). If you want to know what the state of the art is in the scientific study of hypnosis, this is where to find out; it contains a detailed list of references, along with over twenty articles covering all phases of the field. Highly technical.

Ernest Hilgard, *The Experience of Hypnosis* (New York: Harcourt, Brace and World, 1968). The best exposition of the conventional scientific view of hypnosis by its leading authority.

Sarbin and Coe, op. cit. An intellectual *tour de force* providing a definitive rationale for our present approach.

CHAPTER FOUR

Harry Arons, *New Master Course in Hypnotism* (So. Orange, N.J.: Powers Publishers, 1961). The classic text for lay hypnotists, offering a good range of techniques and ideas, although the theory is somewhat outdated.

Barber, Spanos, and Chaves, op. cit. Again, see Chapters 1–8.

William James, *Psychology* (New York: Harper Torchbooks, 1961). First published in 1892, this is where it all began for our approach. See the chapter on habits (pages 1–17).

William S. Kroger, op. cit. Pages 1–84 offer a technical overview of hypnosis and its techniques. Pages 48–49 discuss three of our principles as the "laws of suggestion."

CHAPTER FIVE

Herbert Benson, *The Relaxation Response* (New York: William Morrow, 1975). The best-seller introducing Dr. Benson's findings on the psychophysiological benefits of complete relaxation.

Hans Selye, *The Stress of Life* (New York: McGraw-Hill, 1956). The pioneer of stress research discusses the nature of stress.

Hans Selye, *Stress Without Distress* (New York: Signet, 1974). A more popular volume on how to cope with stress.

John White and James Fadiman, eds., *Relax: How You Can Feel Better, Reduce Stress and Overcome Tension* (New York: The Confucian Press, 1976). A fascinating potpourri of information and techniques related to stress; includes an excellent bibliography.

CHAPTER SIX AND CHAPTER SEVEN

Leslie LeCron, *Self-Hypnotism* (New York: New American Library, 1970). The classic in this field; somewhat outdated, but still probably the most widely read book on the subject.

Freda Morris, *Self-Hypnosis in Two Days* (New York: Dutton, 1975). An interesting, if somewhat far out, book on how to learn a form of self-hypnosis in a weekend marathon. Dr. Morris pioneered the use of making up your own tapes in this volume, an idea to which I am deeply indebted. Her book is particularly slanted toward using self-hypnosis for dealing with academic examinations.

Harry Arons, op. cit. Contains much wisdom regarding how to work with the hypnotic frame of mind. An appendix (pages 200–206) describes Arons's self-hypnosis training approach.

Harry Arons and M. F. H. Bubeck, *Handbook of Professional Hypnosis* (So. Orange, N.J.: Powers Publishers, 1971). Part Two contains an introduction to clinical psychology for lay hypnotists, which may be of value to you. Pages 138–146 and unnumbered illustrations expand upon Arons's self-hypnosis approach cited above. Also contains many ideas for suggestions and visualizations for specific cases.

William S. Kroger, op. cit. Pages 85–90 discuss self-hypnosis.

Maxwell Maltz, *Psycho-Cybernetics* (Englewood Cliffs, N.J.: Prentice-Hall, 1960). A best-seller containing many good ideas useful in self-hypnosis work.

CHAPTER EIGHT

Harry Arons and M. F. H. Bubeck, op. cit. Many specific problem-solving strategies are suggested.

William S. Kroger and William D. Fezler, op. cit. Visualization strategies for all sorts of problems are discussed, with emphasis, unfortunately, upon medical and other clinical applications.

Freda Morris, *Hypnosis With Friends and Lovers* (New York: Harper and Row, 1979). Contains many useful strategies and ideas, from a more "New Age" perspective than my own.

CHAPTER NINE

Lonnie Barbach, *For Yourself* (New York: Signet, 1977). Perhaps the best popular book on female sexuality; contains both information and techniques readily adaptable to use with strategic self-hypnosis.

Theodore X. Barber, Nicholas P. Spanos, and John Chaves, op. cit. Pages 59–126 discuss both issues and strategies related to psychosomatics; especially strong with regard to regulation of blood supply and pain control.

Ernest R. Hilgard and Josephine R. Hilgard, *Hypnosis in the Relief of Pain* (Los Altos, Calif.: William Kaufmann, 1975). Definitive work on the subject.

Dennis T. Jaffe, *Healing From Within* (New York: Alfred A. Knopf, 1980). Good eclectic overview of healing and other psychosomatic potentialities for the general reader.

Gerald Jonas, *Visceral Learning* (New York: Viking, 1973). An introduction to what has been learned from biofeedback.

William S. Kroger and William D. Fezler, op. cit. Contains both background data on the theory of psychosomatics and visualization, and dozens of visualization tactics adaptable to specific needs.

Kenneth Pelletier, *Mind as Healer, Mind as Slayer* (New York: Delta, 1977). Probably the best introduction to psychosomatic medicine for the lay reader.

Bernie Zilbergeld, *Male Sexuality: A Guide to Sexual Fulfillment* (New York: Bantam, 1978). A ground-breaking discussion of male sexuality with many techniques and exercises, all adaptable to strategic self-hypnosis. I wholeheartedly recommend this book.

CHAPTER TEN

Roger Buchanan, "Sports and Hypnosis—Improving Ability," taped presentation from the Fifth Annual Scientific Conference of the International Society for Professional Hypnosis. I wish Mr. Buchanan would write a book about his fascinating techniques, but you can obtain a copy of this lecture or contact him through the I.S.P.H., 218 Monroe Street, Boonton, New Jersey 07005. This is the source for my basic approach to sports enhancement.

Timothy Gallway, *The Inner Game of Tennis* (New York: Random House, 1976). A pioneering book about the psychology of the sport, containing valuable material.

Freda Morris, op. cit. Her two books contain explicit directions for a variety of performance-improvement strategies in both intellectual and physical endeavors.

Maxwell Maltz, op. cit. This classic offers some excellent material regarding motivation for success in many areas of performance, along with good references to other books of related interest.

INDEX